THE ESSENTIAL GUIDE
TO CHILDREN'S
sleep

This straightforward workbook provides clear and targeted strategies to make bedtime easier. Sleep-deprived parents can flip to the relevant chapter and start making changes tonight!

—KRISTEN KALYMON, PhD, BCBA-D, CLINICAL PSYCHOLOGIST, UNIVERSITY OF MICHIGAN, ANN ARBOR

Getting good sleep is so important for kids—it's the secret to doing well in school, making friends, and feeling great emotionally. But let's face it, it's not always easy to come by! With years of experience in childhood sleep, the authors have created a practical, parent-friendly guide to help you build healthy sleep habits for your child and set them up for a lifetime of well-being.

—AIMEE KOTRBA, PhD, COAUTHOR, *OVERCOMING SELECTIVE MUTISM: THE PARENT'S FIELD GUIDE*

As a pediatrician and mom of two I could have used a book like this when my kids were little! Practical evidence-based advice with worksheets to help with implementation. It even has tips on how to deal with the other caregivers who are resistant to sleep training. I recommend this book 100%!

—SARAH LUPU, MD, FAAP, PEDIATRICIAN, CHESTNUT RIDGE PEDIATRIC ASSOCIATES, MONTVALE, NJ

Sleep is essential for every child's well-being, but the path to restful nights isn't one-size-fits-all. This book equips parents and caregivers with evidence-based strategies tailored to every stage and understands a child's unique needs. It's a compassionate, practical guide for families seeking better sleep and stronger routines.

—MONA AMIN, DO, FOUNDER, PEDSDOCTALK

A Tired Caregiver's Workbook
for Every Age and Stage

THE ESSENTIAL GUIDE
TO CHILDREN'S
sleep

ANDREA C. ROTH PsyD
ALLISON SHALE PsyD
SHELBY F. HARRIS PsyD, DBSM

 AMERICAN PSYCHOLOGICAL ASSOCIATION

Published by
American Psychological Association
750 First Street, NE
Washington, DC 20002
https://www.apa.org

Order Department
https://www.apa.org/pubs/books
order@apa.org

Typeset in Sabon by Circle Graphics, Inc., Reisterstown, MD

Printer: Gasch Printing, Odenton, MD
Cover Designer: Mark Karis

Library of Congress Cataloging-in-Publication Data

Names: Roth, Andrea C., author. | Shale Deutsch, Allison, author. |
   Harris, Shelby, author.
Title: The essential guide to children's sleep : a tired caregiver's
   workbook for every age and stage / by Andrea C. Roth, Allison Shale, and
   Shelby F. Harris.
Description: Washington, DC : American Psychological Association, [2025] |
   Includes bibliographical references and index.
Identifiers: LCCN 2024050629 (print) | LCCN 2024050630 (ebook) |
   ISBN 9781433843785 (paperback) | ISBN 9781433843792 (ebook)
Subjects: LCSH: Children--Sleep. | Child rearing.
Classification: LCC BF723.S45 R68 2025 (print) | LCC BF723.S45 (ebook) |
   DDC 154.6083--dc23/eng/20250123
LC record available at https://lccn.loc.gov/2024050629
LC ebook record available at https://lccn.loc.gov/2024050630

https://doi.org/10.1037/0000450-000

Printed in the United States of America

10 9 8 7 6 5 4 3 2 1

CONTENTS

Contents

ACKNOWLEDGMENTS

We thank the anonymous peer reviewers for their feedback.

Dr. Roth also thanks the following: To Justin, Ivy, and Jesse, you make my life both incredibly chaotic and so sweet. To my mother, who taught me how important it was to stand on my own, and my father, Dr. Roth Sr., who gave me the gift of sleep medicine. To my original lady docs and my friends at Thriving Minds, thank you for helping me grow and cheering me on.

Dr. Shale also thanks the following: To J., E., and S., you are truly the best part of every day. Your endless love, support, and understanding will never cease to amaze me. To my parents, who first suggested this career and supported me through the ups and downs of grad school and beyond, you are truly the starting point for all of my success and there could never be enough thank-yous.

Dr. Harris also thanks the following: To my husband, J., you have been an amazing partner in this crazy journey called parenthood and I'm eternally grateful for your love, support, and patience whenever I endlessly talk about sleep. To my son (age 14) and daughter (age 8), thank you for giving me so much more perspective as a sleep clinician. Those early newborn-hood sleep-deprived times had me quite skeptical I could practice what I preached, but I'm glad we all found our groove together and you turned into fantastic sleepers . . . even during these new teenage times when I can't seem to get you out of bed to start the day.

THE ESSENTIAL GUIDE TO CHILDREN'S

sleep

INTRODUCTION

Welcome! We are so happy you are ready to tackle your child's sleep issues and that you are trusting us to help with your precious cargo during what we know can be a difficult time for all involved. Whether you are dealing with early wake-ups, stress-filled bedtimes, or middle-of-the-night difficulties, this workbook will help you feel confident and equipped to tackle these issues.

This book is meant for a variety of caregivers at different stages of childhood sleep. Whether you are the sleep-deprived parent of an infant, the caregiver of an 8-year-old who is experiencing serious sleep anxiety, or the grandparent of an exhausted teenager who is struggling to wake up for school each day, we are here for you.

In this book, we talk a lot about the importance of considering who your child is during the day as part of learning how to tackle their sleep issues. This understanding is particularly important for older children struggling with sleep because you will want to consider how their daytime anxiety or behavioral issues may be part of what you are seeing at bedtime. We also want to be clear from the start that we will not address every possible sleep issue or every possible solution: We focus on the problems we see most often in our clinical practices, and we provide approaches for you to consider when deciding how to respond to what is happening in your home at the time. We take this approach not only because of our experience and training as psychologists, but also because we are always learning about and reviewing the research on sleep. In this book and in our clinical work, we rely heavily on evidence-based strategies (i.e., approaches supported by science and research). Most importantly, we hope that by picking up this book, you can focus less energy on the search for answers to sleep problems because we have done the leg work to provide you with up-to-date guidance. We have narrowed the focus and options to ensure that you don't feel overwhelmed by where to start.

ABOUT US

We, the authors of this book, are all doctoral-level clinicians who not only work with the pediatric population for sleep concerns, but we also specialize in mental health treatment. Our combined, unique qualifications include working with children with anxiety, depression, attention-deficit/hyperactivity disorder (ADHD), obsessive-compulsive disorder, and selective mutism. All recommendations and guidelines presented in this book are based in the same evidence-based practices that we use daily in our clinical work. These specialties make us uniquely qualified to speak on children's distinctive needs as they pertain to sleep.

We all came to this pediatric sleep space in different ways and found each other in equally unique circumstances. Andrea Roth, PsyD, would say that she came to this space by blood and that sleep is truly the "family business." She started by working in a sleep laboratory in Detroit, Michigan, with her father, Thomas Roth, PhD. After working in different positions in different laboratories, she combined this early appreciation for sleep with her passion for research-supported pediatric clinical care in graduate school, where she then met Allison Shale, PsyD. The two then worked together within their clinical placement in Westchester, New York, treating youth with a variety of mental health diagnoses. Their careers evolved side by side, diverging in their clinical specialties, with Dr. Roth going the route of anxiety and depression and Dr. Shale going into behavioral defiance and noncompliance in children. Sleep always kept them together and continuing to collaborate, both in clinical practice and in late-night phone calls over the sleep struggles of their own children.

Shelby Harris, PsyD, was the missing piece of our sleep medicine puzzle. While Dr. Roth was participating in a pediatric sleep supervision group run by juggernauts in the field, Dr. Lisa Meltzer and Dr. Jodi Mindell, she made a passing remark about billing within private practice. An equally casual recommendation to connect with another private practice sleep clinician brought Dr. Roth and Dr. Harris together. Dr. Harris focused on adult sleep throughout her graduate studies; she obtained her board certification in behavioral sleep medicine, directed her own program at Montefiore Hospital, and then created her own thriving sleep practice. With this book, we hope to extend our combined years of knowledge and research-supported sleep interventions beyond our patients and friends, so more families can stop searching for answers and enjoy the benefits of a good night's sleep.

Although our credentials give us a particularly well-educated and informed perspective, our life experiences also ground us in the reality of how difficult childhood sleep issues can be. We are all mothers, and we felt lucky to have each other during the various ups and downs of sleep that our children experienced. Short of getting every one of you into our practices or you having our phone numbers on speed dial, we wanted to provide a helpful resource that you can pick up and put down as needed. We like the workbook format for caregivers because with so little time, so many available resources, and so many challenges in determining reliable sources of information, we know it can be hard to read a book from cover to cover. (If you have that time in the future, we love and recommend Dr. Craig Canapari's 2019 book, *It's Never Too Late to Sleep Train.*) Next, we describe what you can expect from this book.

ABOUT THIS BOOK

By now, you may have talked with friends, family, or even your pediatrician in the hope of finding something (anything!) to increase the amount of sleep your child is getting (which affects your sleep too). As parents and caregivers, we want to make sense of why our children are sleeping poorly or possibly not sleeping at all. Although the recent influx of online and professional advice is helpful at times, it provides a bevy of nonmedical and nonresearched concepts, terms, and approaches for handling disrupted sleep that can be difficult to wade through.

With so many books, podcasts, and websites available, it can be difficult enough to parse out reliable information—let alone try to determine what may be most beneficial for you and your family. Although these different sources of information can be helpful, they often offer a one-size-fits-all approach to sleep solutions. For example, a child who struggles to sleep alone because of anxiety and nighttime fears needs a different approach than a child with ADHD and behavioral defiance. Without a more complete understanding of why your child is not sleeping well and without a targeted plan derived from that understanding, you likely will not be as successful as you could be in addressing your child's needs.

Unlike many sleep blogs and books that make broad suggestions around changing sleep without considering individual differences, the chapters in this book are geared toward a specific age group from infancy through adolescence. Each chapter focuses on the sleep difficulties we have found to be most common at that point in development; when you come to a sleep issue, you can start by reading the age-appropriate chapter. Each chapter includes strategies and brief vignettes that show the techniques in action while also considering possible hiccups and pitfalls. Once you have read about the skills, you can complete a brief worksheet to develop a plan (and backup plans) for self-identified possible problems. Additionally, this book emphasizes identifying your support system. We know that working on sleep challenges can be difficult; having a plan in place with identified people and resources to help you through will increase your chances of success. The worksheets are intentionally brief so you can complete them in a single sitting. This workbook is extremely user-friendly, and no formal knowledge of sleep or complicated medical terminology is required to understand and benefit from it.

It is important that we also mention a few things this book will not do. First, we will not make medical recommendations. This resource will be helpful for a lot of children, but there are some causes of sleep problems that this book cannot address. Some disorders and diagnoses, such as autism spectrum disorder and developmental delays, can complicate sleep issues. In these cases and others, you should consult with a pediatrician or clinical specialist as a first step in addressing and understanding your child's individual sleep needs.

We also encourage you to speak with your pediatrician or another trusted medical professional if your child is experiencing any of the following:

- If you notice that your child is snoring routinely, holding their breath, or gasping for air overnight, this may be a sign of sleep apnea. In this case, talk with your pediatrician about a referral to a pediatric sleep medicine physician or ear, nose, and throat specialist (ENT), because a sleep study might be indicated.
- Although children rarely use the word "restless" to describe their limbs at bedtime, they may say their limbs feel "itchy" or there are "creepy crawlies" on them. They may also say

they have trouble getting comfortable or toss and turn a lot at bedtime. These remarks may be an indication of restless leg syndrome (RLS). It is worth noting that children with ADHD have a higher incidence of RLS than other children (Migueis et al., 2023). To assess for RLS, your pediatrician can perform a simple blood test to measure your child's level of serum ferritin (a protein that stores iron).

• If your child has other medical conditions (e.g., eczema or reflux), we encourage you to get them under control so you can eliminate physical pain or discomfort as a cause of sleep issues.

As mentioned earlier, our approach highlights the importance of considering who your child is outside of their sleep difficulties. We will challenge you to really think about who your child is for the many other hours of the day, because this will help you determine how to best approach their difficulties at bedtime and through the night.

This book is meant to be easy to digest, and we hope you will return to it as needed over time. Rather than read it from start to finish (although you certainly can if you want to look ahead), we recommend starting with Chapter 1 for a review of general principles and guidelines related to sleep. Chapter 1 also highlights reasons to consider a referral for clinical and individualized support and to address medical conditions that can affect sleep, which should be treated first. In the remaining chapters, we discuss the importance of caregiver teamwork (Chapter 2), provide guidance for age groups from infancy through adolescence (Chapters 3–7), and offer troubleshooting tips (Chapter 8).

Throughout this book, we will follow two children, Lena and Nik,[1] from their infant days through their toddler years and beyond.

---

[1]Cases are composites of real clients. Details have been changed to ensure patient confidentiality.

Their stories, and those of their caregivers, demonstrate approaches to resolving sleep issues across various stages of child development and among caregivers with different comfort levels.

We hope that you reference this book throughout your child's sleep journey and that you pay it forward to your friends and family when they inevitably hit a rough patch, too. We think you will feel empowered knowing that you have our guidance in your back pocket whenever you need it.

CHAPTER 1

HOW THIS WORKBOOK WILL HELP YOU ADDRESS A RANGE OF SLEEP ISSUES

You are here because your child is not sleeping as well as you would like, but why is there so much talk about sleep and making sure that children are getting the sleep they need? Many caregivers say they do not know how much sleep their children should be getting, what the appropriate bedtimes are, and what makes a good bedtime routine. Although there is no one approach that fits all, we provide age-specific recommendations in each chapter to take some of the guesswork out of scheduling. In this chapter, we review some general principles and guidelines related to sleep, including the importance of sleep, principles of effective change, and hot topics in sleep medicine.

WHY IS SLEEP SO IMPORTANT?

With the goal of good sleep in mind, we know that inadequate sleep in childhood is linked to many developmental issues. We mention this not to scare you or create panic around childhood struggles with sleep. Rather, it is important to shed light on research regarding poor sleep and health issues to improve understanding. By reading this book because you want to improve your child's sleep, you are already taking an active step to decrease the likelihood of negative outcomes! Read on to simply educate yourself on issues that can be tied to sleep.

First, poor sleep has long been linked to obesity (Beebe et al., 2013), academic failure (Beebe et al., 2010), and increased likelihood of high-risk behavior (O'Brien & Mindell, 2005) and emotional outbursts (Gruber et al., 2012). Following the COVID-19 pandemic, significant and devastating increases in mental health diagnoses (27% and 29% for anxiety and depression) and psychiatric emergency department visits (24% and 31% for children ages 5–11 and 13–17 years) have been reported (Agency for Healthcare Research and Quality, 2022). The link between insufficient sleep and mental health struggles has long been proven for children and adolescents: This is important to note because the recent pandemic had an indirect impact on sleep among these populations by way of mental health. In addition, it is important to remember that poor sleep in childhood affects not only the child but also their parents and potentially the parent–child relationship. Mothers of newborns are particularly vulnerable because poor sleep has been linked to increased rates of postpartum depression and anxiety (Baattaiah et al., 2023). With the importance of sleep in mind, some basic principles should be applied to make effective changes to any child's sleep. We describe these next.

PRINCIPLES OF EFFECTIVE CHANGE

When you are making behavioral changes regardless of whether they are sleep related, consider the following important principles to increase your chance of success.

1. *Consistency and follow-through are important.* If you take only one thing from this book, we hope it is this: Consistency and follow-through are the most important factors in changing your child's sleep or any other behavior issue. You need to be consistent in how you respond to your child, and you need to

follow through on what you say you will or will not do. From a young age, children notice and anticipate how their caregivers will (or will not) respond in a situation: We want your child to know that when you say you are going to do (or not do) something at bedtime, you will follow through.

2. *Set realistic goals and expectations for you and your child.* Your goals and expectations for your child should be realistic and attainable. This book is categorized by age because although children can have sleep issues any time and the issues can have similar causes, how we address these issues and what we expect of children varies widely. Realistic goals make it more likely that you and your child will be successful.

3. *Be patient: Behavior change takes time.* Although we wish we could wave a magic wand and make all children amazing sleepers in one night, remembering that improved sleep takes time will help you better tolerate the ups and downs that come with making changes at home. When we remember how long it took to develop the current "bad" habits, it only makes sense that it takes time to develop new, better habits. Additionally, be kind to yourself: If you have a night that goes haywire, you can (and will) get back on track!

4. *Make one sleep change at a time.* You may find that several topics and concepts apply to your child at any specific time, and it is tempting to want to change everything all at once. We recommend making one change at a time and then waiting 5 to 7 days to determine whether the attempt was successful. When you make one change at a time, you can better tell what is and is not working. For example, if you change your child's bedtime, offer a reward for falling asleep alone, and use compression sheets all in one night, you won't know which aspect was helpful or which one failed. Set your child up for success by making one small change at a time.

SLEEP HYGIENE: SETTING THE STAGE FOR A GOOD NIGHT'S SLEEP

Now that you have some information on creating changes in behavior, let's consider a term you will see throughout this book that is essential to understanding and addressing sleep problems at all ages: *sleep hygiene*. Sleep hygiene is another term for *healthy sleep habits*, and it focuses on both environmental and behavioral factors. Understanding how much sleep your child truly needs is foundational knowledge that leads to improved sleep hygiene. The total number of hours of sleep varies widely for children, just as for adults. The following general ranges are total hours recommended per day, including naps if the child is at an age that still requires them (National Sleep Foundation, 2020). Some children may need more sleep or less.

Age	Total hours of sleep (including naps)
0–3 months	14–17
4–11 months	12–15
1–2 years	11–14
3–5 years	10–13
6–13 years	9–11

An effective and consistent bedtime routine is an important behavioral piece of sleep hygiene, and we will describe its value in nearly every chapter of this book. The main idea is that a good bedtime routine is short, simple, and, when consistent, always cues your child that it is time for bed. The routine should lead to the final goal of sleeping, and it typically comprises three to five activities. Here is an example of a good routine for an infant: put on pajamas, brush teeth, sing a song, and then place the child in their crib. As children get a little older, it can help to make this a visual routine with pictures so they know what is coming next.

Another aspect of sleep hygiene that we will mention repeatedly is the importance of a *positive sleep environment.* When you consider the space where your child sleeps, we recommend keeping the room dark and ensuring that the space is generally quiet (it does not need to be silent). In the early years, many children benefit from the use of a sound machine to muffle outside noise; if you use one, make sure it is at a reasonable volume and not placed immediately next to the crib or bed. In a perfect world, aim to keep your child's room temperature somewhere between 68 and 72 degrees Fahrenheit, which is not too hot or too cold for most. We know it can be challenging to keep the temperature perfectly within the suggested range, especially during warmer months when weather can change drastically during the day and night, and you know your home best. Although many considerations around sleep may feel unpredictable, the environment and the bedtime routine aspects of sleep hygiene are absolutely within your control and establishing them will affect your child's sleep significantly.

We are often asked about screen use before bed. Although there is no clear rule about when or how to use screens before bed, we all agree that screen use should be limited in the hour before bed. In addition, the type of content viewed is in many ways more important than how or when it is watched. Playing video games or scrolling social media will likely be more stimulating than reading a book on an electronic reader or even texting with a friend.

Four actions can improve sleep hygiene for children of most ages (and adults too). Before you read on, know that some of these suggestions may sound idealistic to you or even impossible, whereas others you may already be doing without even knowing that they are helping with sleep. When it comes to some of these broader categories, we find that awareness can be an important first step. Simply paying attention to the lighting in your home before bed or recognizing how many times you do or do not refill your child's water bottle over the course of the day can be eye-opening. It is most beneficial to be realistic about what you can and cannot do consistently. Even picking one or two of these suggestions, as opposed to using an all-or-nothing approach, can be helpful.

1. Maintain a generally healthy lifestyle by providing your child a balanced diet and plenty of drinking water. We are not nutritionists, so we recommend starting with your child's pediatrician to determine whether changes to your child's diet may be helpful for their sleep and overall health.
2. Engage your child in exercise and encourage them to remain active (but see point 3).
3. Reduce vigorous activity close to bedtime as much as possible. We recognize that this can be difficult if your child plays sports or has late activities.
4. Avoid bright lights 2 hours before bed.

TWO HOT TOPICS IN PEDIATRIC SLEEP: MELATONIN USE AND COSLEEPING

Two hot topics in pediatric sleep are melatonin use and cosleeping. Parents are often looking for concrete rules around both, but the research is not definitive. Let's explore what we know about both topics.

Melatonin Use

For various reasons, we will not recommend melatonin in any of our plans. *Melatonin* is a hormone made naturally in the brain's pineal gland, and it takes effect around 2 hours before children and adults become sleepy. Melatonin is commonly referred to as the *hormone of darkness* because it needs darkness to work its magic and help us fall and stay asleep. Melatonin can be purchased in supplement form. Many individuals take melatonin supplements to help with their sleep.

Although we understand that melatonin is truly a godsend for some families, we generally do not recommend it as a first-line strategy for sleep for most children for a few specific reasons. First, melatonin is often unintentionally misused. In fact, the Poison Control Center reported a 530% increase in calls related to melatonin from 2012 to 2021 (Cohen et al., 2023). More is not better when it comes to melatonin; any dose of 5 mg or higher is considered large, despite the routine availability of 10-mg melatonin gummies in stores.

Second, there is sound, current research supporting the use of melatonin as part of a larger sleep plan with specialized populations, including children with attention-deficit/hyperactivity disorder or autism spectrum disorder (Rzepka-Migut & Paprocka, 2020). However, no current research shows the generalizable benefits of melatonin use in the general pediatric population. Additionally, there is not enough longitudinal research that definitively shows the long-term effects of melatonin use in children.

Finally, we do not generally recommend considering melatonin as a first-line response for the majority of pediatric sleep issues. It is often better in the long term to focus on sleep hygiene, such as adjusting a schedule or bedtime routine, coupled with taking a more behavioral approach as outlined in the following chapters. If none of these approaches are effective, consider discussing with your pediatrician whether to add melatonin to your tool kit, along with making behavioral changes. Even then, it is important to check in with your pediatrician regularly about your child's dose of melatonin and whether it is still needed.

Keep the following information in mind when considering melatonin use with children:

- You should always consult your family doctor before using melatonin.
- There is limited longitudinal research on pediatric melatonin use.
- There is little regulation around the production, marketing, and sale of melatonin. According to a 2017 study, the actual dose of melatonin in a product can differ widely from the label (Erland & Saxena, 2017). In fact, comparisons of melatonin content in a supplement suggested a range from 83% less to 478% more melatonin than specified on the label. Equally concerning is the vast discrepancy in melatonin content "between lots of the same product," with variability as high as 465% (Erland & Saxena, 2017, p. 276). That is, if you buy the same brand of melatonin repeatedly, the actual dose you give may differ from bottle to bottle.
- It is recommended that you pick a U.S. Pharmacopeia (USP)–verified supplement. USP verification helps to ensure that the ingredient list is accurate.

Cosleeping

Cosleeping, or bed-sharing, is another hot topic in pediatric sleep (and not just among infants and toddlers). When parents ask about cosleeping, they are often eager for a concrete rule as to whether they should practice it. There are many different thoughts on cosleeping and, in most situations, there is not one correct answer; our general recommendation is that parents can usually continue to cosleep if it is not disrupting their or their child's sleep and, most importantly, if they are doing it safely. When parents say that they enjoy sleeping with their child and that everyone sleeps well and safely, we typically tell them that there is no reason to stop cosleeping. On the other hand, when a parent tells us that they spend half the night tossing and turning because of their child's constant kicking, we often suggest developing a plan to move everyone toward sleeping in their own spaces. In Chapters 3 and 6, we describe a range of strategies that can be used to help your child sleep independently. It is important to note that our recommendations are consistent with those of the American Academy of Pediatrics (AAP). The AAP (2022) strongly discourages bed sharing when children are aged younger than 1 year: To ensure the infant's safety, we strongly recommend the same.

TIME FOR A LITTLE REFLECTION

Now that you have an understanding of the basic concepts in this book and some key topics of relevance for child sleep at all ages, take a few minutes to think about your situation and your motivation to make changes. There are many reasons why people want to adjust sleep: Some are for the child, the family, or the caregiver (or all three parties). There is no right or wrong answer. By considering your "why," we hope you will begin to think about what your family and homelife will look like if your child is getting adequate, undisturbed sleep.

I want to improve my child's sleep because:

_____

_____

_____

_____

(*continues*)

What will change if my child's sleep improves?

_____

_____

_____

_____

Knowing what you have tried in the past to improve your child's sleep, what do you hope to do differently this time?

_____

_____

_____

_____

In this chapter, we reviewed why sleep is important, how much sleep children should get at various ages, and key components to making effective behavioral changes. We also talked about what makes this workbook unique: It looks to identify the root of sleep issues to tailor the plan to attack the problem. Next, you can turn to the chapter that covers your child's current age and start reading! You can also visit Chapter 2 to learn more about the importance of caregiver teamwork in your efforts. Remember, there are worksheets in each chapter, and it can be helpful to review them first to get an idea of the types of questions you will be looking to answer as you read.

We also recommend that you formally track your child's sleep while you attempt to make sleep changes, because this helps you not only gather some initial data but also observe patterns. A log with instructions is provided in Table 1.1, which you can copy and use over and over. We hope that this is the start of a successful sleep journey. Good luck!

TABLE 1.1. Sleep Log

	Day						
	1	2	3	4	5	6	7
1. What time did your child go to bed? *At bedtime, what time did they turn the lights out and attempt to sleep?*							
2. Did they wake during the night? *List all night wakings and each duration.*							
3. What time did they wake for the day?							
4. Did they nap? *If so, at what time and for how long?*							
5. Notes *Note any additional, relevant details here (e.g., medication, caffeine consumption, changed location, etc.).*							

CHAPTER 2

GETTING ON THE SAME PAGE: THE IMPORTANCE OF CAREGIVER TEAMWORK

Some families are fortunate to have two or more caregivers involved in raising their child. People say it "takes a village" to raise children. When parents, grandparents, babysitters, or other caregivers are in the picture, attempting to coordinate sleep changes across all village members can be difficult. It is important to ensure that everyone involved in your child's sleep is on the same page before implementing sleep changes; anyone who helps with bedtime or nap time, even if infrequently, should be included in this group. In our experience, this is a bit easier said than done. When it comes to parenting, it is difficult to find two (or more) people with identical parenting beliefs. As adults, we all have different temperaments and childhood experiences, so it makes sense that we would also respond to children's individual personalities differently. With this in mind, it is common for caregivers to be in different camps in terms of what they think is right and wrong when it comes to sleep and sleep training. We find this to be true for all types of families, whether married, divorced, separated, or multi-generational, to name a few. The goal is to find common ground so all members of the caregiving team can get on the same page. Although the good cop/bad cop trope is longstanding, we have come to learn that consistent messaging between caregivers yields the best results. So, how can multiple caregivers get on the same page?

A VILLAGE OF CAREGIVERS

In our practices, we often tell families to allow space for everyone's opinions and then get educated. This means you go into the process ready to listen to others, validate all opinions, and then do your best to find a middle ground that puts the child's well-being at the forefront, even if that means shifting your viewpoint and considering an alternate approach. In our opinion, the best way to find that middle ground is to get educated and to allow research and recommendations from trained professionals to be your guide. Reading this book is a good start. If you need additional support, consult with your pediatrician, a sleep specialist, or a psychologist. Having an outside party present to offer facts and act as a sounding board can be immensely helpful. We often serve in this role when it comes to two-caregiver households trying to decide on how to move forward in their sleep work; we present research and data, and allow caregivers to talk through the choices and come to a decision that feels right for everyone involved.

Getting on the same page can become further complicated if a child shares time between different households, perhaps because of a divorce, separation, or shared time with grandparents or other family members. Although the households are different, consistency remains important. Caregivers cannot force ex-spouses (or even spouses) to parent the same way they do, so establishing some foundational similarities can be helpful. Caregivers have some say over many factors of a child's sleep, such as when and where they sleep and how they respond to the child's resistance. Picking some lower hanging fruit that is less emotionally fraught, such as the sleep schedule, might be a good place to start. If caregivers can settle on this one small thing, they are helping their child immensely and this may help build toward more consistency in the future. We also cannot state enough how helpful it can be to get support from a therapist who specializes in coparenting.

Finally, let's talk about grandparents and in-laws. They mean well, but they also often have big opinions. They raised you and you are great, so how can their opinion be wrong? They watch your children for free, so how can you disagree? This is another moment to be sure to listen, respect everyone's opinion, and present facts. Again, with grandparents and in-laws, it may be helpful to start with simpler actions, such as the sleep schedule, as opposed to trying to get them on board about how you may respond (or not respond) when sleep training. How often your child is with family or other caregivers can also help you decide what is and is not worth a fight.

As we mentioned earlier, you will get to know two children over the course of this book as we show how various approaches look in practice. First, let's meet Lena.

Lena was 7 months old when her parents presented for treatment. Lena struggled to sleep through the night, and her parents were considering sleep training. Lena's sleep village had a lot of players, including her parents, grandparents, and twice-weekly day care. Everyone had their days with Lena: mom had one day, dad another, grandma another, and day care the remaining two. Lena's dad felt ready to begin some form of sleep training, but her mother and grandma felt that forcing Lena to cry in order to learn to sleep was cruel and that she would eventually figure it out herself. To further complicate matters, Lena napped two times a day at home, and day care continued to offer three naps.

At their intake appointment, Lena's parents provided a lot of information about Lena's sleep and overall temperament. In turn, they received a great deal of psychoeducation, or education, about sleep and intervention. They learned about infant sleep, how it evolves and changes, what is viewed by research as optimal sleep and its benefits, as well as the variety of ways they could sleep train their baby, not just the assumed cry-it-out method. Afterward, they took time to discuss their opinions, worries, and goals. They were able to reach a consensus and form a sleep plan for Lena. They were provided this plan in writing and advised to call a family meeting with grandma to present their decision and take the time to explain why it was important. They were encouraged to provide her with a copy of the written sleep plan as well.

Having everything in writing and accessible to all parties involved in the child's sleep is the linchpin of all these plans. Complete Worksheets 2.1 and 2.2 to get on the same page with your child's caregivers and to create a sleep plan.

WORKSHEET 2.1. Getting on the Same Page

While you complete this worksheet, spend some time thinking about your parenting style, your child's overall mood and temperament, and your home environment. By writing things down and being proactive (instead of reactive) about possible issues, you will be more likely to follow through on the plan that you are setting. Remember, you can always return to an earlier part of the chapter for a refresher on a specific skill.

1. Who is on my child's caregiver sleep team?

   _____

   _____

2. What are we currently good at doing consistently and as a team?

   _____

   _____

3. Which aspects of our child's sleep do we most disagree on currently? (Consider timing, location, cosleeping, and middle-of-the-night responses.)

   _____

   _____

4. Is there one smaller aspect of the listed items that we can be flexible and agree on to start with? An example would be the bedtime schedule.

   _____

   _____

5. Is there an outside person, such as a specialist or counselor, who can help us come to an agreement?

   _____

   _____

WORKSHEET 2.2. Our Sleep Plan

This worksheet is meant to be used over and over as you read this book, as a way to communicate with all caregivers and stay on the same page. You may not be ready to complete this sleep plan yet, but come back to it when needed. Ideally, you will have multiple copies of this plan for all caregivers and display it prominently so all can stay in the loop.

1. This sleep plan is for (your child's name): _____

2. Bedtime is: _____

3. Where does the child sleep?

   _____

   _____

   _____

   _____

4. The bedtime routine includes:

   _____

   _____

   _____

   _____

5. If the child struggles to fall asleep or protests at bedtime, our planned response will be:

   _____

   _____

   _____

   _____

6. If the child wakes during the night, our planned response will be:

   _____

   _____

   _____

   _____

(continues)

WORKSHEET 2.2. Our Sleep Plan (*Continued*)

7. The child should be awake by this time: _____

8. If they wake earlier than we would like them to, our planned response will be:

_____

_____

_____

_____

Naps (If Applicable)

1. The child's naptimes are: _____

2. If the child wakes in the middle of the nap, our planned response will be:

_____

_____

_____

_____

3. If the child takes a very short nap or skips a nap, we will adjust by:

_____

_____

_____

_____

4. We plan to wake the child at a certain time or limit the length of a nap by:

_____

_____

_____

_____

THE VILLAGE EXPANDS: DAY CARE AND SCHOOL

Many children attend day care or some type of school program in their early years. Day care and school can be wonderful experiences for young children that allow them to socialize and learn outside the home. If your child is age 5 years or younger and attends a program, odds are that some form of rest or naptime is at least offered during the day. Some children adapt to this different sleep space easily, and others struggle a bit more with the changed setting. Young toddlers who sleep in a crib in a dark room at home begin to sleep on a cot in more light at day care. By and large, we are very impressed with how positive peer pressure helps even the most nap-resistant toddler sleep during the day. There is something miraculous about seeing 12 toddlers all cooperatively walk to their cots and lie down when prompted!

There are common times for infants and toddlers to drop naps (read more in Chapter 4), which can be affected by day care schedules. We commonly hear about what feels like a premature drop to one nap at age 1 year in many day care facilities. This drop naturally tends to occur a few months later for children who nap at home consistently. Although this drop may not feel ideal to caregivers, our general recommended rule of thumb is this: Whoever puts the child down for a nap most often during the week is the one who sets the schedule. In other words, if your child is napping at day care 5 days a week, the timing there sets your schedule at home. Rather than continue to offer your child two naps on the weekends, mirror the day care schedule of one nap at home as well. It may feel difficult or your little one may be more tired at first, but this is short lived and can typically be remedied with a temporary early bedtime.

Attempting to make a change in the nap duration can be another hiccup when your child is most often napping outside of the home. In our experience, many facilities are typically happy to collaborate with families in their sleep plans. Occasionally, some day cares are beholden to company or state regulations, making their nap policies rigid and intractable. We have worked with families whose children are in day cares that require offering a nap to children through age 5 years. What "offering a nap" means to some day cares can starkly contrast with what it means to others. Can the child simply sit on their cot with an activity, or do they need to be in the dark lying down? Sometimes, it can be helpful to shorten a nap or even cut it completely when the child is age 3 or 4 years, especially if it is significantly interfering with their ability to fall asleep at bedtime. We know that consolidated overnight sleep is more restorative for a child than daytime sleep, so it can be helpful to prioritize it. We recommend that you schedule time to sit down with your day care teacher, and possibly the director, to discuss your desired change and explain why you want to go this route. It can be helpful to join them in troubleshooting their concerns, which are typically around where the child will go during naptime or what they will be allowed to play with.

> Getting Lena's parents and grandma on the same page was a huge victory, but the work was not done. Lena's parents were encouraged to request that their day care match their two-nap schedule at home. Initially, the teacher was resistant and insisted that the day care must offer as many naps as the infant appeared to need, which seemed more like a company policy than a recommendation. Lena's parents were then instructed to schedule a more formal meeting with the teacher and the director of the day care. Just by taking this step, the day care became more flexible, and both the director and the teacher indicated that they would be happy to trial offering Lena two naps at day care. Within 2.5 weeks and with everyone on the same page, Lena was sleeping through the night and consistently taking two naps per day.

CHAPTER 3

SURVIVING THE FIRST YEAR

Congratulations on your new bundle of joy! These days, one of the first questions people may ask you upon meeting your baby is, "How are they sleeping?" The answer often becomes the metric for how a baby is doing overall. There is a lot of pressure around sleep, and there are a lot of opinions about the best method to get your baby to sleep through the night. In this chapter, you will learn about safe sleep guidelines, how to help your infant get their recommended amount of sleep, and how to help yourself get the sleep you need during this exciting year.

In subsequent chapters, we will focus a great deal on the why behind your child's sleep difficulties. This chapter is a bit different because we want to normalize the fact that infants wake during the night. Early on, babies are not waking due to behavioral issues; instead, they often wake due to typical infant development. As they get closer to age 6 months, infants may struggle to stay asleep due to sleep associations, or actions they require to fall asleep, such as nursing or rocking. It is hard to say how many infants will have these associations and how many will just know how to sleep through the night. The research varies widely and indicates that as low as 54% and as high as 84% of 6-month-olds sleep through the night (defined as hitting a 6-hour stretch; Pennestri et al., 2020). Later in this chapter, we address these very normal sleep associations and talk about ways to improve your child's ability to self-soothe and sleep independently. Of course, if your baby has reflux or a complex medical condition, please discuss sleep training with your doctor before beginning.

In 2022, the American Academy of Pediatrics (AAP) updated its safe sleep guidelines focused on positioning, bed-sharing, and pacifiers, among other topics. Moon (2022) summarized the guidelines as follows:

- *Sleep surfaces:* Use a flat, noninclined sleep surface. A crib, bassinet, portable crib, or play yard should conform to the safety standards of the Consumer Product Safety Commission.
- *Sleep location:* Infants should sleep in the parents' room, close to the parents' bed but on a separate surface designed for infants, ideally for at least the first 6 months.
- *Bed-sharing:* Although the AAP cannot recommend bed-sharing based on the evidence, it also respects that many parents choose to bed-share routinely for a variety of reasons.
- *Bedding:* Do not place any soft objects, including pillows, blankets, or bumper pads, in the infant's sleep environment.
- *Pacifiers:* Pacifier use is associated with a reduced risk of sudden infant death syndrome (SIDS).
- *Monitoring devices:* Home cardiorespiratory monitors [or a wearable item that typically tracks heart rate and oxygen levels] should not be used to reduce the risk of SIDS.
- *Tummy time:* Supervised tummy time should start soon after hospital discharge and increase slowly to at least 15 to 30 minutes total daily by 7 weeks of age.

In the 2022 update, the AAP stood by its previous recommendations around the importance of placing an infant to sleep on their back on a flat surface and avoiding bed-sharing, in addition to highlighting that pacifiers can reduce the risk of SIDS. However, the AAP made some noteworthy changes: Most important were warnings against the use of many common products, including weighted swaddles and sleepers, and home breathing and heart monitors not approved by the U.S. Food and Drug Administration. Finally, although the AAP still supports having a parent room-share with their baby, they reduced the recommended length from 1 year to just the first 6 months of life. In this chapter, all recommendations will strictly adhere to the AAP (2022) guidelines.

SURVIVING THE FIRST 10 WEEKS

Newborn babies sleep about 14 to 17 hours each day (often divided equally between day and night). Their sleep occurs in shorter periods to accommodate feeding, diaper changes, and interacting with family. Some interesting and helpful differences improve understanding of newborn sleep versus sleep in later infancy. Newborns have *quiet sleep* and *active sleep*. Many parents think their newborn is uncomfortable, awake, or in distress when they observe them grunting or moving around in their sleep; however, this is completely normal, active sleep. During active sleep, your baby might startle themself awake; this is why it is recommended to swaddle your new baby to help reduce these awakenings. Newer swaddles have options including arms tucked in, up, or out and, as with all sleep recommendations, no one size fits all. You may need to experiment to find what your baby does best with.

Through the first 10 to 12 weeks of infancy, it is normal for your baby to wake during the night, most likely for feedings and diaper changes. Younger infants also wake during the night because they do not yet have fully developed circadian rhythms. You may know a bit about circadian rhythms or have just heard the term.

Circadian rhythms are the body's 24-hour cycle of regulation based on light and dark. Simply, circadian rhythms are the body's internal clock and help us sleep in the dark and stay awake in the light.

Newborn babies can get overtired very easily, so it is important to keep the following in mind:

1. Have appropriate expectations! The number one sleep problem encountered in early infancy is a mismatch between parental expectations and what can be realistically expected from a newborn. Although your neighbor or second cousin may have had a baby who slept through the night at 3 weeks, this is not the norm. Young babies are meant to wake during the night, and anticipating this will help you feel less frustrated when it happens.
2. When babies are born, they do not know the difference between daytime and nighttime. Day/night confusion is common but, fortunately, it can be remedied. You can provide daytime awake cues to your baby by having lights on and using a louder voice during the day. During the night, even during feedings and diaper changes, lights and voices should be low because you want the baby to understand that it is nighttime, which is meant for sleep and not playtime. Additionally, for that first daytime morning feed, it can be helpful to move the baby to a different setting outside of the bedroom to signal that daytime has begun.
3. It is never too early for a bedtime routine, as this too can help with day/night confusion. A brief bedtime routine at the end of the day can signal bedtime to your baby. Here is an example of an infant bedtime routine: bath, massage, book, then bed. It is most important to do the same things in the same order each night.
4. It is important to always look for your baby's sleepy signals and try to get ahead of tiredness. Babies use different signals to

show they are getting tired, including rubbing their eyes, fussing, tugging their ears, or even looking away from you. Noticing these signals can make it easier for you to successfully put your baby down at the right time so they can fall asleep most easily.

Surviving the First 10 Weeks: The Fast Facts

- Have appropriate expectations: Young infants are meant to wake throughout the night to feed and have their diaper changed. Most importantly, they simply wake because they are infants! This stage will pass eventually.
- Day/night confusion is common: You can combat this by using light exposure and activity levels (volume and setting) to your advantage, such as increasing light and talking at a normal volume during the day and using low light and whispering at night.
- Your baby is never too young for a bedtime routine: Even in the first days of your baby's life, you can create a brief bedtime routine at the end of your day. Remember, bedtime routines should be brief and follow the same sequence each night.
- Younger infants sleep a lot and get tired easily: To avoid your baby becoming overtired, watch for their signals, including eye and ear rubbing, fussiness, and looking away, so you can put them down at a time that makes it easiest for them to fall asleep.

Lena was a sweet newborn baby whose parents sought support early in their infant sleep journey. As the first couple in their friend group to have a baby, they reported not knowing what to expect or what to do. They walked away from one session armed with information on newborn sleep, better understanding of what to expect, and a few tips to help Lena sleep a little better. After their session, they began to use more cues at nighttime with Lena during feedings. Previously, Lena's dad was taking her downstairs to the fully lit living room to watch television while he fed and changed her. He learned to stay in her dimly lit room and listen to podcasts on his earphones while he fed her, which helped him stay awake. Additionally, they began putting Lena down for naps a little quicker than before, rather than allowing her to show more significant signs of getting overtired, like crying and eye rubbing.

Throughout this chapter, we will watch Lena age. We will also observe how her parents survive the first year.

BRIDGING THE GAP: 10 WEEKS HAVE PASSED, SO WHEN SHOULD YOU SLEEP TRAIN?

Your baby is now no longer a newborn but is still not old enough to sleep train. You can see the light at the end of the sleepless tunnel, but you are not quite there yet. By now, we hope you have a nice bedtime routine in place and that initial day/night confusion is a thing of the past. Instead of feeling helpless and hopeless as you wait for your baby to successfully sleep through the night, you can do some things to prepare to sleep train. Because their circadian rhythms are now more strongly developed, babies tend to do better on a set (by-the-clock) schedule. The current focus on wake windows, or how long an infant has been awake for, goes against what we know about infant sleep architecture at this age. Although there should always be wiggle room in our schedules, babies will do better if we begin to set their sleep schedule for them, much like we do for our own healthy sleep as adults.

Naps, bedtime, and location are important to consider at this age. Each is described next.

- *Naps.* At this age, babies typically take three naps per day: one in the morning, one in the afternoon, and one in the late afternoon or early evening. All naps should be finished by 4:30 p.m. to prevent interference with bedtime. Here is a schedule example: 9:00 a.m., 12:00 p.m., and 3:00 p.m. (Note that some babies are chronic short nappers, rarely stretching beyond 30 minutes at a time; generally, these babies should go down for naps every 2 hours, as opposed to every 3 hours in this example.)
- *Early bedtime.* Most infants are ready for bed around 7:00 to 7:30 p.m. Contrary to what many people believe, bedtimes later than 8:00 p.m. can result in overtiredness, which often leads to more night wakings or earlier rising (Mindell et al., 2015).
- *Location, location, location.* Ideally, your baby should be sleep trained in their final sleeping location. If you plan for them to sleep in a crib for the next few years, move them to the crib now to prepare for sleep training. Keep the room cool, dark, and quiet with white/brown noise, and keep using that previously created bedtime routine!

In the newborn days, you probably often rocked your baby to sleep while either holding them in your arms or moving them in some way (i.e., in a stroller or swing). For example, you may have worn your baby as you completed tasks around the house, or you went for a walk while pushing your snoozing baby in the stroller. As babies get older and as you begin to feel more comfortable, we want you to slowly introduce your baby to more independent sleep.

Start by attempting to put the baby down for sleep while they are drowsy but awake. Doing so allows them to attempt to fall asleep independently. Because you are not formally sleep training, you can absolutely pick your baby up to soothe them if they become upset. In this stage prior to sleep training, remember to walk but don't run when your baby makes noise or fusses at wake time. That is, take your time in getting to your baby when you hear them over the monitor: Give them an opportunity to impress you and potentially fall back to sleep without your help.

Bridging the Gap: The Fast Facts

- Schedule: Babies do better with by-the-clock schedules at this age. Generally, they should be napping three times per day (in the morning, early afternoon, and later afternoon or early evening), with all naps finished by 4:30 p.m. to not impact bedtime.
- Bedtime: Research shows that young children do better with earlier bedtimes (Mindell et al., 2015). Aim to have your baby in bed before 8:00 p.m. to avoid them becoming overtired.
- Drowsy but awake, and walk but don't run! Give your baby a chance to practice sleeping independently. Try occasionally putting them down while they are drowsy but awake, and don't rush to get them the moment they stir. They may surprise you and possibly even fall back to sleep without your help.

When Lena was 15 weeks old, her mom reached out for support because her husband was back to work and traveling quite often. To cope, Lena's mom began religiously tracking Lena's wake windows during the day and following strict associated recommendations that she found online. Even with this, Lena was only taking brief, 20-minute naps all day long until she was put to bed. In this session, it was determined that the wake windows were not helping and obsessing over them was making Lena's mom miserable. Shifting to a nap plan that followed the clock, rather than how long Lena had been awake for, allowed Lena and her mom to have a little more regularity and predictability in their day. They also shifted bedtime a bit earlier to ensure that Lena did not get overtired.

Lena's mom did not feel that she would want to sleep train, so she declined the recommendation to pause before immediately responding to Lena when she woke from sleep.

SLEEP TRAINING

If you have a baby, you likely have heard about sleep training by now. You have also likely heard many opinions on this topic. In our experience, these opinions tend to be black and white: People are usually either keenly for sleep training or strongly against it, and there is little gray area. Historically, sleep training was viewed as simply the act of using behavioral strategies to help a child sleep independently. When sleep training was introduced in the 1800s, it was an approach to help babies sleep a bit more and be more scheduled; it certainly was not as controversial as it is today. Most people against sleep training assume that it requires you to let your infant cry alone for hours on end; social media, influencers, and self-proclaimed parenting experts have amplified this assumption. One thing we can all agree on, regardless of background or training, is that getting more sleep is important for your baby and the entire family.

Decisions on how you raise your baby, including whether to sleep train, are very personal. Rather than sleep train, some families prefer to cosleep or to continually and directly help their children fall asleep and stay asleep throughout the night. If either approach is done safely and all family members feel satisfied, we will not disagree. Rather than simply state "You do you," we provide the following take: As clinicians, we strive to do right by our patients and their well-being and, personally, we choose to allow science and research to guide our decisions on how to practice. We will follow this framework throughout the book, beginning with sleep training. We will not disparage other perspectives or opinions or state whether they are right or wrong. We will present our recommendations along with data to support them. With that said, we open this section by addressing the metaphorical elephant in the room: There is no peer-reviewed literature that validates the idea that sleep training your infant will cause any emotional damage in the short or long term. There is, however, extensive research that supports long-term gains from improved infant sleep (Pennestri et al., 2018; Tham et al., 2017). One of the largest studies on sleeping training was conducted by Hiscock and colleagues (2007), in which 300 children who were either sleep trained or not were followed for 6 years. Notably, there were no significant differences in the two groups' behavioral concerns, several years after sleep training in infancy. There also were no significant differences in the children's cortisol levels, which is the stress hormone that opponents of sleep training frequently point to. Finally, by age 2 years, the children who were sleep trained were actually sleeping better than their non–sleep-trained counterparts and their mothers were less likely to be depressed, a point that should not be overlooked!

Before you begin sleep training your infant, many preliminary details are worth noting. Although infants are typically ready to sleep train between 4 and 6 months, we cannot solely judge their readiness by age. First, you should confirm your infant's readiness to sleep train with their pediatrician because they can review information such as your infant's feeding in addition to their weight gain and growth. You should also wait to see signs of self-soothing, which is one of the best indicators for readiness. Does your baby put their hands or thumb in their mouth? If they become upset during the day, what do they do? Look for these daytime self-soothing behaviors. There are a few red flags that let us know that a baby is not ready to sleep train (yet!):

- If your baby is sick, do not start sleep training.
- If your baby is actively teething, it may be best to begin after teething stops.

- If your baby is still in a swaddle, they are not yet ready to sleep train. Remember, you should stop swaddling if your baby is rolling or even close to rolling; we want them to be able to move their arms so they can roll safely and freely.
- Most importantly, if you are not ready to sleep train your baby, do not start! We know that sleep training can be harder on caregivers than on infants. There is a varied but expected amount of crying that may come with sleep training, and it is not right for all families. If it does not feel right to you, then don't do it!
- Similarly, if one parent wants to sleep train and the other does not, we recommend discussing fears and hesitations with your pediatrician. In some situations, the parent interested in sleep training will simply take the lead while the other parent does not participate as actively.

If your baby is between age 4 to 6 months and you have determined that you both are ready for sleep training, we want you to be aware of a few more changes. At this point, you are probably noticing that your baby is beginning to sleep a little bit less over the course of the day, which is to be expected. We begin to see babies averaging closer to 12 to 15 hours of sleep per day at this age. Their circadian rhythms are more strongly developed at this point: This means they are likely associating nighttime more with sleep and sleeping more hours in a row. but they are also possibly waking a bit more often in the night as they cycle in and out of sleep. Again, all of these changes are to be expected.

SLEEP TRAINING APPROACHES

Once you have settled your baby into a consistent routine and determined that you both are ready to sleep train, it is time to pick an approach. Three primary methods are outlined next: extinction,

4 1

modified extinction, and parental presence. All are effective. Read about each next, and think about what best aligns with you and your family.

Extinction (Cry It Out)

Extinction (*cry it out*) is the most well-known version of sleep training: You follow your standard bedtime routine, place your baby down in the crib at the end of the routine, and then do not return until your chosen wake time in the morning. Always go into your baby's room if you are concerned for their safety or if there is a medical reason. Most research indicates waiting until your baby is age 6 months to use this technique (Hiscock et al., 2007). Additionally, if your infant has experienced abuse or neglect, we do not recommend this option.

Modified Extinction (Checking Method)

Modified extinction is also known as the *checking method* or *Ferber method*. You will also follow your standard bedtime routine, place your baby in bed while they are drowsy but awake, and then leave the room. If the baby starts to cry, you check on them at set intervals. These intervals can either be fixed (e.g., every 5 minutes) or graduated (e.g., checking first at 5 minutes, then at 7 minutes, and so on). Checks should be brief and boring, lasting no more than a minute or two. During these checks, you can pat and shush your baby but do not pick them up. These checks continue until your baby falls asleep.

Parental Presence (Camping Out)

Research indicates that *parental presence* may be the slowest approach to sleep training (Honaker et al., 2018), but it can be comforting to parents who are more nervous about the process. As we said earlier, your readiness and comfort are incredibly important, and being mindful of what you can and cannot tolerate will help you pick an approach that can more easily lead to success. With the parental presence method, you follow your bedtime routine and place your baby down while they are drowsy but awake. You then stay with your baby and comfort them in their crib by patting, shushing, and offering brief verbal reassurances. After 3 to 5 successful nights (meaning there is limited crying and your baby is falling asleep in the crib), you physically move yourself halfway between the crib and the doorway after you place your baby down for bed. You can continue to verbally comfort your baby, but do not touch them. Next, after another 3 to 5 successful nights, move to the doorway. The final step is for you to move out in the hallway after the final 3 to 5 successful nights. Some parents transition out even slower, moving away by 2 to 3 feet every few nights, especially for larger bedrooms. You may also have heard people use the newer term, *camping out*, in reference to this.

Having three options to consider feels simple enough, right? Most often, caregivers want to know which method they should select or which works best. Unfortunately, there is no one-size-fits-all answer because one method is not empirically better than the others. However, some guidelines and considerations can make choosing easier: Extinction is like ripping a bandage off, with more discomfort up front but quicker resolution. Checking might feel more progressive but labor intensive. Finally, parental presence is slower but can be comforting to parents who struggle to not be near their crying baby.

The best method for your family is the one that fits not just your infant temperamentally but also you as a caregiver. If you have a partner in parenting, you should also think about whether you want to both participate or if it would be better for one of you to take the lead while the other provides support. It is most important to pick a method you know you can stick with consistently: Beginning sleep training and then quitting partway through is not only upsetting but also reinforces your baby's crying, as they begin to learn that their caregiver may cave and rescue them if they get upset at bedtime.

Finally, you must decide whether you want to sleep train your child for daytime and nighttime sleep at once or separately. The field of pediatric sleep medicine is split on which path to travel. Some argue that if you can ride a bike in the morning, you can ride a bike in the evening. Or in this case, if you can teach your baby to fall asleep independently at bedtime, they should be able to carry this through to the middle of the night and for naps. Anecdotally, sometimes this works and sometimes it does not. Consider this question: Do you want to take it slow and steady, or do you just want to be done? Research indicates that when we begin to sleep train, we see significantly reduced crying in 3 to 4 nights and completion within 2 weeks when using either extinction or modified extinction (Honaker et al., 2018). Regardless of which method you choose, you will ultimately need to decide on a realistic *okay-to-wake time* for the morning. For example, if your baby typically wakes at 5:00 a.m., shooting for 8:00 a.m. might not be realistic. Most families settle somewhere around 6:00 to 7:00 a.m. and use their sleep training strategy at bedtime and then again overnight until the chosen wake time. If you choose to go piecemeal, it is recommended to start with bedtime, then shift to the middle of the night after 3 to 5 nights of success, and then tackle naps after 3 to 5 more nights of success.

Nap Training

Again, at this age, your baby should be napping about three times per day in the morning, afternoon, and late afternoon or early evening, with all daytime sleep finished by 4:30 p.m. Contrary to popular advice, you should also wake a napping baby after they have been asleep for 2 hours. Overly long naps reduce sleep pressure for the next nap or at bedtime. To nap train, use the same sleep training method (extinction, modified extinction, or parental presence) to put your baby down for their nap. Once the baby wakes, give them a chance to self-soothe for about 15 to 20 minutes. Full extinction for this short time (i.e., not going in at all) works best; if you are not comfortable doing that, use your preferred sleep training strategy for these 15 to 20 minutes. If your baby does not sleep at all for their nap, get them out of bed and either try again in 20 minutes or bump up their next nap time (or bedtime) by about 30 minutes.

Troubleshooting Sleep Training

Caregivers typically raise a few common concerns when considering sleep training. The first is room-sharing with a baby. If you room-share with your baby, you can begin to sleep train just at bedtime because they likely go to bed before you. When logistically possible, some caregivers choose to move out of their bedroom for about 2 weeks while they sleep train, then move back in once they are done.

Second, the crying baby may wake an older sibling. If they are sharing a room, the older sibling may try moving out of the room for 2 weeks (if possible) until sleep training is done. If this is not an option, consider adding a sound machine. Your home may start to sound like a fan factory, but it is helpful to have a sound machine in the hallway between bedrooms (in addition to within the bedrooms) to buffer all noise. Although many people assume that older children are light sleepers, many sleep deeply and you may be surprised by what they can sleep through.

Finally, sometimes infants cry so hard that they vomit. This is relatively uncommon, but have spare bedding and pajamas ready for your baby if this occurs. Sometimes it can be helpful to use layered sheets so you can quickly remove the dirty set without having to put new ones on. If your baby vomits, stay calm and do not overreact. Go in, quickly and quietly change your baby and the bedding, and place them back in their crib for sleep while they are drowsy but awake. Remember to keep voices and lights low.

45

PACIFIERS

We are commonly asked what we think about pacifiers during a baby's first year. We know that pacifier use is empirically proven to reduce the incidence of SIDS (Moon et al., 2012). Some babies love pacifiers and others hate them. Some kids are soothed by pacifier use, even overnight. The next question is whether parents can use pacifiers during sleep training. This answer is a bit complicated. If you often return to your little one's room to replace their pacifier, the pacifier is likely not conducive with sleep training. We do not want your baby to rely on you to retrieve the lost pacifier. However, if your infant can put their own pacifier in, go for it! You can help them with this skill by using hand over hand and practicing the movement of pacifier to mouth during the day and leaving several pacifiers in the crib. In accordance with AAP (2022) recommendations, note the following: At this age it is only safe to have plain pacifiers, without attached stuffed animals, in the crib. Otherwise, we recommend dropping the pacifier early on when you are ready to begin sleep training. In our experience, the next window to drop the pacifier generally does not occur until your child is closer to age 3 years (as we discuss in Chapter 4).

Sleep Training: The Fast Facts

- Ensure that both you and your baby are ready to start sleep training: It is important for both of you to be ready for sleep training; consider your child's temperament, and speak with their pediatrician.
- Choose one of three methods: Extinction is the most widely discussed approach, which involves allowing your baby to cry it out until they fall asleep. You place them down while they are drowsy but awake and do not return until their designated wake time. With modified

extinction, you check on your baby at scheduled time intervals, either fixed (e.g., every 5 minutes) or graduated (starting at 5 minutes, then 7 minutes, etc.), if they begin to cry. Parental presence keeps a caregiver in the room at specific locations the entire time while the baby falls asleep.

- Decide if you want to go all in or piecemeal: There is no right way to sleep train. Pick an approach that will allow your family to be most consistent. Choose your okay-to-wake time and decide if you want to take small steps to sleep train or rip the bandage off, attacking daytimes and nighttime sleep at once.
- Nap train: Your baby should be taking three naps at this point and, ideally, their schedule is based on the clock. Use your chosen sleep training method at their designated naptimes, and then allow them to try to self-soothe upon waking and fall back to sleep.

Lena, now 7 months old, presented to treatment with several night wakings and brief, 30-minute naps. Her parents were exhausted and at odds with each other around how to handle her sleep. Her father was adamant about letting her just cry it out, while her mother did not like the idea of sleep training altogether. After they received a great deal of psychoeducation about infant sleep and behavioral intervention, Lena's parents settled on using modified extinction to help her sleep more.

Before Lena's parents could even begin working on modified extinction, they were instructed to initially change a few small sleep habits. First, they were allowing Lena to nap three times across the day, with her final nap being at 6 p.m., making bedtime close to 8:30 p.m.; her naps were shifted forward so that they could be finished by 4:30 p.m. Additionally, Lena's mother was nursing Lena as the last step in her bedtime routine, and Lena nursed until she fell asleep. Instead, Lena's mother was encouraged to nurse at the start of their bedtime routine to ensure that

Lena went to bed drowsy but awake and with less dependence on nursing to put her to bed. Finally, her parents added black-out curtains to the bedroom to eliminate much of the sunlight that crept in during naps.

Once Lena's parents felt ready and Lena's mom returned home from a 3-day work trip, they began the process of modified extinction at bedtime, deciding to wait to address naps separately. They opted to start with brief intervals of just 2 minutes in the first night, and they eventually increased to 15 minutes. Lena displayed significantly decreased crying and sleep latency (or time to fall asleep) in just 5 minutes by 6 days into training. On day 9 of sleep training, they shifted their strategy to the middle of the night; by this time, she was only waking once or twice during the night, and this resolved within 3 additional days. Finally, 3 days later, they tackled naps.

It is important to note that Lena and her parents lived in a one-bedroom apartment in a city, and they had been sleeping in the same room as Lena. They elected to move out of their bedroom and slept on their pullout sofa while they sleep trained. They moved back into their bedroom with her 1 week after she was sleeping through the night.

Are you ready to form a sleep training plan? Complete Worksheet 3.1 to develop one.

WORKSHEET 3.1. Sleep Training Plan

While you complete this worksheet, spend some time thinking about your parenting style, your child's overall mood and temperament, and your home environment. By writing things down and being proactive (instead of reactive) about possible issues, you will be more likely to follow through on the plan that you are setting. Remember, you can always return to an earlier part of the chapter for a refresher on a specific skill.

1. Which sleep training method will I use?
   – Extinction
   – Modified extinction
   – Parental presence

    – I think this method will be a good fit for both me and my baby because:

_____

_____

    (It will help you to write out a sentence about why you and your baby's temperaments align with your chosen strategy. Doing so helps you make the most appropriate choice and remain consistent.)

2. How do you want to approach this?
   – All in
   – Piecemeal (start with bedtime, then overnight, then naps)

3. What is my child's okay-to-wake time? _____

4. Take a moment to write some general notes about your plan. Think about ideal bedtimes, who will do what, which intervals will you use for checks (if you select that strategy), and so on.

_____

_____

5. Who will support me in these steps?

_____

_____

6. I would like to complete these steps by this date: _____
   (Is there anything that will stop you from starting right away, such as a trip?)

7. My backup plan(s):

_____

_____

What do I think could go wrong? Do I anticipate any barriers that could make it harder for me to follow through with my plan?

_____

_____

If this happens, what can I do? Should I keep moving forward or pause training? Who can I ask for help?

_____

_____

NIGHT WEANING

Regardless of your child's age, you likely remember numerous night wakings in those early infant days. Newborns tend to be ravenous upon waking because their tiny stomach only holds a small amount of nutrition. Fortunately, as newborns grow into infants, toddlers, and beyond, they remain better satiated overnight if they are growing and getting sufficient nutrition during the day. Although some babies are ready and able to sleep in 8-hour stretches by age 4 to 6 months, some continue to wake during the night. It is important to consider whether your baby is waking because of actual hunger or if they are in the habit of feeding to soothe and settle back to sleep. As a first step when considering dropping an overnight feed (or feeds), we always recommend talking to your pediatrician about your child's growth. It is important to ensure that your child is growing appropriately and that they are healthy and grown enough to handle a longer stretch without eating. Second, as we have repeatedly stated, you need to feel ready to make this change. If you enjoy night feeding and feel that it is quick and helpful to your baby, you do not need to rush to drop the night feed. Most parents hit a point, although at different times, at which they feel ready to reclaim a longer stretch of sleep for themselves, and this typically triggers them to broach the topic with us.

Although *weaning* is often considered in relation to breast feeding, here we use the term in reference to stopping all overnight feeds, whether breast, bottle, or both. As with all things sleep related, you can take a variety of approaches to weaning—some more gradual than others. Before you address night weaning, take a minute to think about the purpose that feed serves (e.g., resolving hunger vs. responding out of habit or comfort). We first want to break the feed-to-sleep cycle at bedtime and naptime so there is less reliance on feeding to put the baby to bed initially. Here are some simple steps:

Move the bedtime bottle earlier in the bedtime routine, and feed the baby in a room other than the bedroom if possible. If you feed the baby in the bedroom, keep the lights on to avoid cuing bedtime with the introduction of food. A routine might look like this: pajamas, bottle, books, songs, then bed. The goal is for the feed to not be the last step, so the baby is not falling asleep while eating (and then needing to eat to fall back asleep overnight).

No matter which approach you choose, it is important to plan for how you will respond to overnight wakings now that feeding will not be your go-to. If you have already done some form of sleep training, you may want to think about what worked for you then. If not, take a moment to think about your own tolerance for crying: Most children will protest night weaning to varying degrees, so setting yourself up for success in carrying out your chosen plan will be most important. As we highlighted earlier, there are three common approaches to respond to your baby:

- Extinction (cry it out) is the most common and involves allowing the baby to cry until they fall asleep. After your normal routine, put your baby down while they are drowsy but awake. Do not go back in their room (unless there is an emergency) until the next morning when it is time to wake for the day.
- Modified extinction (checking method) also involves putting your baby down while they are drowsy, but instead you check on your baby if they start to cry. These checks are done at scheduled intervals that are either fixed (e.g., every 5 minutes) or graduated (e.g., first at 5 minutes, then at 7 minutes, and then at 10 minutes).
- Parental presence (camping out) means you stay in the room until your baby falls asleep. The key is to position yourself in planned locations in the room.

Once you decide how you will respond to your baby, consider the night-weaning approaches described next, which focus on the feed itself as opposed to your baby's response. Regardless of the approach you choose, it is helpful to start on a weekend or a night where you have more flexibility the next day, in case you and your child are more tired from the change in overnight routine.

Systematically Decrease Ounces Fed or Minutes Nursed

One night-weaning method involves slowly decreasing the number of ounces you feed (or minutes you nurse) until you eliminate the feed entirely. For a few days before you plan to start, make note of how long your child nurses or how many ounces they eat. You pick the pace, but we often recommend dropping an ounce (or 1 to 2 minutes) every couple of days until you eventually get down to zero. Many parents share that although this pace is gradual, some babies feel upset or confused by not getting to eat until they are full. Again, having a prepared response will help you follow through with your plan. It is important to also note that sometimes your baby will jump ahead and eat less than you offer. For example, maybe your baby is eating 4 ounces, but one night they only eat 3 ounces. Going forward, only 3 ounces should be offered because we know the baby can be satiated with that amount.

Focus on the Clock

You can focus on the time of night you feed your baby (vs. the amount they eat) and then gradually push that time out later until you reach morning. Again, take a few days to track what time your baby wakes overnight. Here is an example: Your baby often wakes around 12:30 a.m. Starting on day 1, you will not feed your baby if they wake any time before 12:30 a.m. because you already know they can make it to that time on many nights. Although the hope is they naturally wake after that, use your sleep training tools to determine the response you will give if they wake before your identified new feeding time. Consider these questions: What can you do to hold the baby off until their new feeding time? Would gentle shushing or offering a pacifier work? You can go into the room if that is part of your decided approach. At some point, your baby will sleep later. Let's continue with our example: After a few days, the baby sleeps until 1:15 a.m. Now that the baby has successfully slept until 1:15 without a feed, this becomes the new feeding time. You will continue to push the time out later when your baby reaches a new time. As the time gets later and therefore closer to your desired wake time, you can self-select and use those sleep training methods again to get them through the wake up without a feed. If baby does not stretch the time on their own, push the time out by 15 to 20 minutes every couple of days.

Go Cold Turkey and Pull It All at Once

Once your pediatrician says it is okay for your child to drop the overnight feed, some caregivers find it easiest to pull the feed entirely (i.e., go cold turkey). This does not mean you cannot respond to your child if they wake overnight, although some caregivers decide to pull both the feed and their response at the same time. Your comfort should be the biggest determinant of whether that approach is right for you and your family. The benefit for some caregivers is that this is typically a much faster approach to adjustment and eliminates the feed entirely. Use Worksheet 3.2 to establish your plan for night weaning.

WORKSHEET 3.2. Night Weaning

When it comes to night weaning, regardless of whether you are breast or bottle feeding, it is important to have a plan for how you will respond to your baby's night wakings. No matter which approach you take to weaning, there will likely be some amount of protest from your baby who has gotten used to being fed until full overnight.

1. I will start night weaning on: _____

   (Remember, select a weekend or a day that would be slightly easier to tolerate if you and your baby are more tired.)

2. I would like to complete night weaning by: _____

3. Who will support me in these steps?

   _____

   _____

4. I will try one of the following strategies for night weaning focused on feeding:
   – Decrease ounces fed or minutes nursed
   – Focus on the clock
   – Go cold turkey

5. Sleep training methods can be helpful. (Remember that the best method is the one that fits both your baby and your temperament!) I will try one of the following strategies:
   – Extinction (cry it out)
   – Modified extinction (checking method)
   – Parental presence (camping out)

6. What is your current bedtime routine?

   _____

   _____

   Does the feeding need to be moved earlier to break the relationship between feeding and falling asleep? _____

WORKSHEET 3.2. Night Weaning (*Continued*)

7. My backup plan(s):

_____

_____

What do I think could go wrong? Do I anticipate any pushback from my child or another caregiver? Do I anticipate any barriers that could make it harder for me to follow through with my plan?

_____

_____

If this happens, what can I do? Should I stand strong or pivot? Who can I ask for help?

_____

_____

CHAPTER 4

TAMING TODDLER AND PRESCHOOL SLEEP

You did it! Congratulations on making it through the first year. In doing so, you likely found a sleep training strategy that worked for you, and you saw the fruits of your labor in having your little one successfully sleep through the night. This is a huge milestone, and you should celebrate that win!

Just as you are getting comfortable in your new normal, your child becomes a toddler and may be suddenly fighting bedtime. Kids keep us on our toes! Your toddler may start running around as soon as bedtime is mentioned or refuse to let you change their diaper. They may cry for you, need another lovey or hug, or climb out of their crib or bed. With toddlers and preschool-aged kids, changing how we respond to these behaviors tends to help change what they are doing. In this chapter, we focus on rewarding and reinforcing behaviors we want to increase, such as our child willingly going to bed, staying in their crib all night, or not calling for us repeatedly. At the same time, we also consider the benefit of sometimes providing consequences for behaviors we want to decrease, such as ignoring repeated calls for us.

First, we discuss how to respond to behavioral issues related to sleep. Then we focus on common, difficult transitions that are often encountered before age 5 years. Examples include changing nap schedules, decreasing the number of naps per day, or shifting to a toddler bed; any of these can derail sleep progress. In our clinical practice, difficulties that result from these changes can be the reason parents come to us for help. Here is the good news: Concrete strategies can be used to help you and your child in this stage (just as in infancy). Finally, we will discuss three nighttime issues also seen at this age: sleep terrors, sleepwalking, and bed-wetting.

Before you read further about ways to reinforce positive behaviors, it is important for you to review Chapter 1. Pay particular attention to how to set a solid bedtime routine and establish a positive sleep environment.

Now, consider how your toddler's current sleep difficulties began. Take into account how they behaved and how you responded and adjusted. Finally, reflect on some of your child's other qualities that are important to consider when making a sleep plan.

What sleep difficulties are you facing, and when did they begin? Which behaviors seemed to start this change?

_____

_____

How have you, as a caregiver, been reacting and responding to these behaviors? Were your responses effective, even if just temporarily?

_____

_____

Now, quickly jot down some notes about your child's temperament. Is your child flexible or rigid? Are they easygoing or stubborn? Are they outgoing or more reserved?

_____

_____

Finally, look for some daytime clues. If your child participates in a child care program or you have consistent routines at home, how does your child respond to them? Do they follow them with ease or push back?

_____

_____

BEHAVIORAL APPROACHES FOR YOUR YOUNG CHILD

When we try to get children to change a behavior they've had for many weeks, months, or even years, we often must find a way to get their buy-in—especially if they do not want to change a behavior that is working for them. For example, your child may think it is fun to get in and out of bed or to call for you 10 times. With this in mind, a simple reinforcement plan can be an easy (and realistic!) way to reinforce good behaviors.

Behavioral Rewards and Reinforcing the Good

Parents often use complicated or long-term reward plans with their toddlers. Let's consider the example of getting children to dress independently each morning. Many days, they put on their underwear and rely on you to do the rest. To entice them to do more, you offer a reward (e.g., a toy they really want), but they can only have it if they dress themselves completely 7 days in a row. Although this is a nice goal, going from underwear to perfection in a week is unlikely for a toddler. A more reasonable goal would be to add one more article of clothing at intervals (e.g., maybe every 2 or 3 days). This goal is attainable in terms of both capability and feasibility; we want our toddler to be successful early on so they feel motivated to do even more. If a task is too difficult from the start, many kids give up entirely, feeling hopeless that they will ever be successful.

Toddlers and preschoolers require more immediate or simplified reward schedules. With regard to sleep, we recommend providing a simple reward each morning based on the previous night's behavior. Think of a small reward that you would not mind giving your child each day but would still be special to them. Common examples are a single small piece of candy or a sticker offered at breakfast.

When parents come to us, they often say they do not want to bribe their children or create situations where their children expect rewards for everything they do. However, research has shown that external rewards do, in fact, translate into internal motivation (Bear et al., 2017). It is important to remember that rewards are given after the desired behavior, whereas bribes are given before it. Say you take your child to the supermarket: If you give your child candy immediately because they promised to listen, they may be less likely to do so because they have already gotten the treat. If you say you will reward their listening once you get to the check-out line, they will be continually motivated to listen as you move through the store. The same goes for sleep: Offering the treat at bedtime for the promise of a good night's sleep is a bribe. Offering the treat in the morning, after the child has completed the hard task, is a reward they have earned for their effort. Regardless of motivation, they completed something that has been difficult for them in the past. Use of a reward plan should be temporary, and we do not expect you to need to offer a reward every morning indefinitely. The reward serves as an initial external motivator, and you can eventually phase it out as your child's internal motivation grows.

We understand that some people are uncomfortable with the idea of using any incentive to lead to behavior change. We typically suggest that families give behavioral rewards a try: If this approach does not work, you can try something else. In our experience, most families realize that a very small reward can be a temporary way to get their child on board in doing something that might be difficult for them to internally motivate themselves to try. We do not suggest that you buy large toys or offer lavish gifts. Often, the best rewards are spending time with a caregiver, reading extra books at bedtime, or maybe even allowing bonus screen time when children are a bit older. We suggest that if you buy a reward, it should cost no more than $5. The point of rewards is not to give your child the most amazing gift; rather, you want to help them over that initial hurdle so they will try a new skill or behavior. The hope is that as your child's success builds, their positive feelings (and all that praise you will be giving them, which we talk about next) become the reinforcer. Initially, you may offer a reward every day, then maybe every 3 days, then every week; eventually, your child will not need the reward to do that task. Think about potty training, which many parents feel comfortable with rewarding: You may have given a little candy or a star for each time your child went to the bathroom. Again, you gave this reward after they went to the bathroom (as opposed to before). Your now successfully potty-trained child likely does not ask for a candy each time they go to the bathroom. You naturally phased out the external reward and your child's internal motivation to go to the bathroom took over.

In addition to a simple reward plan, you can use *labeled praises* at any time or place because they only require your attention and your words, making them easy to use consistently. Using labeled praise means you specifically identify what your child did that was positive or helpful. Instead of a general praise, such as "Great job!" try this: "Great job listening!" or "Great job coming to your room so quickly!" These examples specifically tell your child what they did well, help them clearly see the things they can get good attention for, and reinforce the behavior, making it likely that they will want to repeat it to get the same good attention. We recommend you start using these labeled praises throughout the day to give attention to the good (while ignoring the bad, which we talk about next). The hope is that by reinforcing generally good behavior throughout the day, these actions (e.g., listening and following directions) can generalize to bedtime. Here are some additional examples of labeled praises:

- I love when you [help clean up]!
- Thanks so much for [listening the first time]!
- You're so good at [sharing]!
- Great job [putting on your pajamas quickly]!

Parental Attention and Planned Ignoring

Although you are giving your child lots of praise for good behaviors with the intention of increasing those actions, there are likely also behaviors you would like to decrease. Before you learned about labeled praise, you may have been tempted to leave your child be if they were doing what they were supposed to do. Then, as soon as you heard something less desirable brewing in the other room, you likely jumped into action and were corrective and attentive to their misbehaving.

It seems to make sense that addressing undesired behaviors would help to reduce them, but we know that this approach can have the opposite effect. Any attention, even "negative" via lectures or corrections, can unintentionally increase less than desirable behaviors. Attention is attention, whether positive or negative—especially at nighttime. Therefore, the best way to improve behavior is to give children more attention when they are doing something you like, such as using labeled praises, and removing your attention when they are doing something you dislike. This is particularly important during the bedtime routine. Young children tend toward stalling behaviors during this routine through overt tantrum behaviors, subtler complaints, and many tactics in between. What seems like an innocent "I am not tired yet" can turn into a full debate on why your child looks sleepy or why sleep is important. Next thing you know, 10 minutes have passed, and they have successfully distracted you! We encourage you to work hard at ignoring all these minor bids for attention, and only focus on forward movement with the end goal being sleep. This is a great opportunity to use a labeled praise for any step taken toward bedtime (e.g., "Wow, you got your pajamas on lightning quick!").

Behavioral Approaches for Your Young Child: The Fast Facts

- Providing behavioral reinforcement via praise and small rewards can help increase desirable bedtime behaviors (e.g., staying in bed at bedtime): For this age group, it is important that rewards are small and immediate. Toddlers and preschoolers struggle to understand and remember long-term or complex reward systems. Offering something small (e.g., a small candy or sticker each morning) based on the previous night can be exciting and positively reinforcing. Labeled praises are an easy way to highlight anything positive during the bedtime routine: These can be thought of as full-sentence praise, in that it is important to praise a specific behavior ("Good job putting on your pajamas so quickly!" rather than "Good job!").
- At the same time, try not to engage with your child over each small, negative behavior (e.g., minor bids for attention or denying sleepiness), so you do not inadvertently reinforce the bad stuff: Focus your attention on helping your child move through the bedtime routine, ignoring anything that distracts from the end goal of independent sleep.

Next, we introduce you to Nik and his parents. We will follow their sleep journey throughout this book.

> Nik was a 2.5-year-old boy who "hated bedtime," according to his parents. They indicated that things had taken a turn for the worse about 3 months ago, when he transitioned from his crib to a toddler bed after successfully climbing out of his crib on numerous occasions. They reported that when bedtime was announced, Nik would run and fight until they got him into bed. He also required one parent to sit next to his toddler bed to ensure that he stayed put and went to sleep.
>
> Before Nik's parents made any significant sleep changes, they were instructed to begin shaping his behavior both during the day and at bedtime by ignoring his small bids to delay bedtime while also working to praise his compliance and flexibility. Additionally, Nik's parents used a visual timer to help him move through the bedtime routine, and they gave him a sticker for meeting the expectation each night. The timer was initially set for 30 minutes, much longer than he should need, and eventually decreased to just 15 minutes. Providing this larger time window in the beginning increased his buy-in.

Complete Worksheet 4.1 to identify behavioral approaches you will use to shape your child's behavior.

WORKSHEET 4.1. Behavioral Approaches for Shaping Behavior

While you complete this worksheet, spend some time thinking about your parenting style, your child's overall mood and temperament, and your home environment. By writing things down and being proactive (instead of reactive) about possible issues, you will be more likely to follow through on the plan that you are setting. Remember, you can always return to an earlier part of the chapter for a refresher on a specific skill.

WORKSHEET 4.1. Behavioral Approaches for Shaping Behavior (*Continued*)

1. I will use the following strategies from this chapter:
   - Behavioral rewards and labeled praise
   - Parental attention and active ignoring

2. Who will support me in these steps?
   _____
   _____

3. What specific behavior would I like to see my child engage in more (e.g., listening the first time I ask, trying something out of their comfort zone and being brave, being flexible, and so on)?
   _____
   _____

4. What rewards would I like to use for my child?
   _____
   _____

5. Is there a smaller behavior that I would like to start actively ignoring from my child (whining, passive procrastination, etc.)?
   _____
   _____

6. How do I think my child will respond to active ignoring?
   _____
   _____

7. How can I stand strong if they push back?
   _____
   _____

8. I would like to complete these steps by this date: _____

   (Is there anything that will stop you from starting right away, such as a trip?)

TOUGH TRANSITIONS: NAP CHANGES AND TODDLER BEDS

The toddler years are filled with many changes, several of which are related to your young child's sleep. The two biggest sleep changes are transitioning from a crib to a bed and decreasing the frequency of naps (and eventually eliminating them altogether). Let's start by focusing on the crib-to-bed transition, as so many parents ask about this one.

Very often, parents share that they "had" to change their child to a "big-kid bed." There are a variety of reasons for this transition: Parents need the crib for another baby, their child seems too big for the crib, their child asks for a big-kid bed, and, most often, their toddler has found a way to climb out of the crib so the transition is needed for safety reasons. Although any of these reasons may push caregivers to make the switch, it is important to consider whether the child is developmentally ready to have the freedom that comes from an open sleep space like a bed. Research indicates that it is best to wait until a child is at least age 3 years to transition from a crib to a bed (Williamson et al., 2019). At age 3 years, children have improved impulse control and are not as reliant on the physical prompt of the crib slats to remember to stay in bed. They are also more likely to respond to behavioral strategies that are targeted at keeping them in bed. Before age 3, many young children struggle with understanding that there are "imaginary" boundaries (e.g., the sides of a crib) in a bed that should keep them there throughout the night.

When you and your child are ready to make the move to a toddler bed—and we mean both of you—we recommend using a good-morning light. Many fancy models are available, but you can use any light with a timer. Our budget-friendly recommendation is an outlet timer used alongside any nightlight. About 1 to 2 weeks before you make the switch, begin setting the light for your predetermined okay-to-wake time. It is important to set a realistic wake-up time. We would all love to sleep in until 9:00 a.m. but if your child typically wakes at 6:45 a.m., a light is not going to make sleeping in until 9:00 a.m. happen. As we discussed in earlier chapters, most families land somewhere between 6:00 and 7:00 a.m. as their daytime wake time.

It is very important that you introduce the good-morning light while your toddler is still in a crib. Remember what we said earlier about behavior plans? The same applies here in that we want that buy-in and success right from the start: Make it easy for them to stay in bed until the light comes on by having it in the crib without an escape route. You will introduce the light by telling your child that it will turn on when it is time to wake for the day. On day 1, when the light goes on, go into your child's room to retrieve them from their crib and use a simple phrase such as, "Light's on, time to get up" or "Light is on, Mommy is here." This helps them start to create the link between the light and the start of the day. If we are working in reverse and you have already switched your child into a toddler bed and they are waking with the sun, we can still implement a good-morning light to help rectify this. For about a week, record the time your child wakes (say it is 6:00 a.m., on average). To get your child on board with the idea that they cannot immediately jump out of bed when awake, we want them to feel immediate success. Meet them where they are, and then work from there. You want to initially set the light slightly before their typical wake time; for our example, we would start at 5:45 a.m. since they are usually up by 6:00 a.m. Whenever they stay in bed until the light comes on, you will offer one of those small rewards, like a sticker. Then start shifting the time later, by about 10 minutes per day, while continuing to reward staying in bed until the light comes on, until you have hit a more doable and realistic okay-to-wake time.

Keeping Your Child in the Crib

We typically say there is no such thing as a sleep hack, and we encourage you to focus on consistency and follow-through for longer-term success. However, when it comes to the crib-to-bed transition, we have two recommendations that can help to keep your child in the crib until they are more developmentally ready:

- *Sleep sacks are not just for infants.* Sleep sacks also come in larger sizes. We recommend looking for sleep sacks that resemble zippered sleeping bags rather than sacks with individual legs. The sleeping-bag style makes it harder for the child to successfully lift their leg over the side of the crib to jump out; this is often enough of a deterrent for many kids, enabling everyone to sleep longer. Did you use a sleep sack in the past but your toddler figured out how to take it off? Flip it around so the zipper is in the back—yep!
- *Patience is your friend here.* Infants who learn to hang out in their crib in the morning tend to become toddlers who also don't mind waiting a bit to get up once they wake. Keep using that walk but don't run mentality even after they are sleeping through the night (for a refresher if needed, see "Bridging the Gap" in Chapter 3).

Nap Transitions

Regardless of where your toddler is sleeping, transitioning from two naps to one and then eventually to no nap can be very scary and overwhelming. The drop to one nap often occurs around age 14 to 17 months, and dropping the nap entirely can happen any time between age 3 and 4 years. Remember, these are averages and not hard-and-fast rules; no two babies are exactly alike when it comes to their sleep needs.

If your little one is somewhere near the windows just described and is skipping more naps than not, go ahead and drop the nap. Remember, if you realize you moved too quickly and your toddler still needs a nap, you can reintroduce the nap and try to drop it again in a few months. When dropping from two naps to one, you can slowly push back the start time of the morning nap (remember, you are scheduling based on the clock) until the second nap naturally drops. Another approach is to go cold turkey and immediately downshift to one nap, dropping the morning nap entirely and shifting the start time of what used to be the second nap. If your child is on a mostly traditional sleep schedule and waking between 6:00 and 8:00 a.m., that single nap will likely fall somewhere between 12:00 and 1:00 p.m. When you are first dropping to one nap, start it a bit earlier (as early as 11:00 a.m.) to help with the adjustment of no longer getting that first nap because they are closer together. You may observe that at first your child is still taking a shorter nap at just an hour or maybe even a little less. This is okay, as they will quickly gain some nap stamina and most kids eventually learn to sleep for longer; however, while the nap is still short, put your child to bed a bit earlier too to avoid them getting overtired. Refer to the nap training section in Chapter 3 to help guide you in your attempts to get your little one to nap longer.

The drop from one nap to no nap is the tougher transition for most babies. We frequently observe that between age 3 and 4 years, the nap goes from the thing that holds your child together to the thing that completely wrecks bedtime, seemingly overnight. That is, at some point, too long of a midday nap will reduce your little one's sleep pressure at night, so much so that it can take them hours to fall asleep at bedtime. Once we begin to observe this pattern, it is important to either reduce the length of the nap or drop it altogether. Again, you can either ease into this by progressively shortening the nap or you can go cold turkey and drop it all at once. We recommend putting your child to bed a bit earlier while they adjust to this change as well.

Although rest does not substitute for sleep, it can be helpful to offer your child *quiet time* or *rest time* once they have dropped napping. This break allows everyone to recharge their batteries for the second half of the day. Starting small—maybe just 15 minutes and working up to an hour slowly, and possibly with a reward—is a good approach. Providing specific toys or activities to your child for this time is also helpful.

Finally, in clinical work, we are often asked the following question around nap changes: "What do we do when our child is in full-time day care and their schedule is different from ours at home?" We suggest that whoever puts the child down for nap most often during the week is the one who sets the schedule (refer to Chapter 3 for more). So, if your child is napping at day care 5 days a week, set your schedule at home to follow suit. Many families have shared that their day cares drop a child down to one nap around a year of age. Although this is not ideal, most toddlers can adjust to this and do fine! Keeping a consistent sleep schedule across settings, as with everything else, helps to keep naps on track.

Tough Transitions: The Fast Facts

- Transitioning your child from a crib to a toddler bed is not a decision to be made lightly or reactively: Research indicates that it is ideal to wait until at least age 3 years to transition your child to a toddler bed (Williamson et al., 2019). At this age, they are better able to understand the concept of staying in bed and have the self-control to do so without the walls of the crib reminding them. In addition, using a good-morning light can help ease the transition, particularly when paired with a small reward for staying in bed until the light comes on.
- Although there are no magic ages for dropping naps, toddlers tend to drop from two naps to one between age 14 and 17 months and then go to no nap between age 3 to 4 years: These transitions can be done gradually or cold

turkey. Regardless of your approach, using a slightly earlier bedtime can be helpful during these acute moments of transition. If your child is in full-time day care, it is important to make nap schedules between home and day care as consistent as possible. Your child's nap schedule should be based on whatever setting they nap in most often during the week.

THUMBS, PACIFIERS, AND STUFFIES, OH MY!

We briefly discussed pacifier use in Chapter 3, and we recommend either dropping a pacifier within your child's first year or waiting until they are closer to 3. We recommend not trying to drop the pacifier at 18 to 24 months because preschool-aged children are better able to understand the process and be more willing participants. Around age 2, your child feels many things but may not be able to really articulate them or understand what is happening. With this in mind, we want to do whatever we can to make this transition as easy as possible; in most cases, waiting really pays off in the long run. Many families opt to trade their child's pacifiers for a small toy or donate them to the pacifier fairy, a magical being that comes and trades you pacifiers for treats. We have even seen caregivers use a pacifier tree, where little kids tie their used pacifiers to the tree and bid them farewell. Do we, as psychologists and sleep specialists, have strong feelings about pacifiers and thumb sucking at this age? You may be surprised, but the answer is no! Pacifier use is a personal conversation for you and your child's dentist. Stuffed animals (or stuffies), on the other hand, can be wonderful for sleep and we are on board with their use, within reasonable limits. As long as your child's bed does not turn into an overly distracting zoo of animals, stuffed animals can be a good transitional object and source of comfort. They allow for children to have a sense of familiarity when they sleep away from home, whether at day care or on vacation.

GETTING BACK ON TRACK

You have learned about handling tough transitions such as dropping naps and changing to a big-kid bed, but what if the wheels have come off and your beautifully sleep-trained infant now won't stay in a toddler bed? (We feel for you and have been there ourselves!) Remember that this is okay and is to be expected as your child is growing, developing, and learning. Try to remind yourself that good sleep is a skill we need to keep practicing and fine-tuning, even far into adulthood. Let's break this down into three simple steps: sleep hygiene, bedtime, and overnight.

Sleep Hygiene

Hopefully, the bedtime routine you established for your infant (Chapter 3) has grown with you and your child and still fits nicely into your family's evenings. The bedtime routine should still be brief, consisting of completing about three to five tasks and heading toward bed. For example, say the bedtime routine for your infant used to be pajamas, bottle, book, then bed. Maybe it looks like this for your toddler: brush teeth, pajamas, book, then bed. This routine should stay as consistent as possible each night and always move toward the bedroom or bed.

Now let's talk timing. Research has shown that younger children tend to do better with earlier bedtimes, such as getting into bed by 8:00 p.m. Although this might feel like a sacrifice for some families, we think it can be important to remember that this phase in life is short and there is wonderful evidence to support good sleep habits throughout childhood and even adulthood that are born in age-appropriate bedtimes (Mindell et al., 2009). Finally, in the hour or two before bed, it is important to be thoughtful about a few things—namely, light exposure and activity level. Bright lights from the sun or even screens can block the production of melatonin, that wonderful chemical that makes our littles ones sleepy (Chapter 1). Try to limit bright light as much as you can, within reason, in the hour before bed. The same goes for physical activity levels! If your child tends to be more energetic, let them get those wiggles out before bed, but do so at the very beginning of your routine so they can shift gears by bedtime.

Bedtime

If your sleep habits are solid and your child still struggles to fall asleep without you, it is time to make a few more changes. It is very important to note right now that while you work on bedtime, we prefer that you leave the middle of the night alone for just a little while, even if your child is calling for you or coming into your room. It is best not to take on too much all at once: Slow and steady will win this race. At this point, you can lean on some basic sleep training strategies you used with your infant—namely, parental presence and modified extinction (Chapter 3). Remember, the basics always apply: Just modify them a bit to meet your child where they are developmentally.

- *Parental presence.* With this strategy, you will gradually shift yourself out of your child's room at bedtime. Every 3 nights, shift your position in their room from next to or in their bed to halfway out of the room, in the doorway, then outside the door. If your child is anxious, you can add a stop or make the shift every 4 days instead. It is more important to create the plan up front and stick to it.
- *Modified extinction.* Similar to infancy, you will say goodnight to your child and then immediately leave the room. Pop back in to quickly and quietly check on them until they have fallen asleep. The time intervals between checks should be set and increased each night. Again, for an anxious little one, you can use shorter

checks in the beginning; we have started with intervals as short as just 30 seconds!

Our last note for bedtime revisits the behavioral reinforcement section at the beginning of this chapter. The strategies just described will be more successful when they are paired with a labeled praise at bedtime or even a tiny prize or sticker in the morning. On the other hand, if your child complains or even gets out of bed, walking them back with minimal to no engagement will help extinguish the behavior.

Middle of the Night

Now that your child is falling asleep independently at bedtime, they may have magically stopped waking in the night. Probably not! We find it easiest to repeat your bedtime method in response to any overnight wakings; we recommend waiting about 2 weeks after mastering bedtime before you try to tackle middle-of-the-night waking. If your child is out of bed, walk them back to their room and use parental presence or checks until they fall asleep. A simple phrase ("It is time for bed") is helpful, but say it in very matter-of-factly without sounding angry or frustrated (remember, that's reinforcement, too!). Typically, once children learn that the plan is here to stay and they will no longer be sleeping with you, the behavior will decrease and likely disappear. Again, we will always have greater success when we pair this new compliance with a small reward and labeled praise.

Getting Back on Track: The Fast Facts

- Sleep hygiene: The bedtime routine should be brief and headed toward bed. Try to maintain an age-appropriate

> bedtime prior to 8:00 p.m. Avoid caffeine, physical activity, and bright light in the hours before bed.
> - Bedtime and middle of the night: Lean back into parental presence or modified extinction first at bedtime and then in the middle of the night. Pair this with behavioral reinforcement for greater success!

Once Nik was moving through the bedtime routine with greater ease (of course, not perfection), his parents used parental presence at bedtime. They set stations next to his bed, halfway across the room, next to the door, and outside the door (Nik slept with the door shut, so the doorway was not an option). They chose to take things slowly and steadily, as Nik was described to not like change, and moved stations every 5 days. Nik earned a mini marshmallow each morning when he stayed in bed until he fell asleep.

BED-WETTING

Any undesirable experience that can occur while we sleep is called a *parasomnia*. We will discuss parasomnias in depth in Chapter 5, but bed-wetting (enuresis) is relevant here because this topic arises frequently when we talk with parents of younger children. It is important to note that parasomnias are entirely out of your child's control and are not behaviorally induced. There is no typical age of bed-wetting onset, as it can be normative throughout early childhood; pediatricians tend to have differing opinions on when bed-wetting becomes concerning. Although some parents are alarmed when it happens, overnight accidents can still be incredibly common between ages 5 and 7. Many pediatricians even say that bed-wetting only becomes problematic once the child thinks it is, likely when they want to attend their first sleepover. However, if it is time to treat your child's bed-wetting, there are a few routes you can take. First, help train the child's bladder by having them void regularly and then stopping liquids in the hour before bedtime. There are also many highly effective bed-wetting alarms on the market. These alarms go under your child's sheet, sense wetness, and prompt your child to get up and use the bathroom. If these strategies do not work when used consistently, you can consult your pediatrician and consider medication.

Complete Worksheet 4.2 to plan how you will tackle these tough transitions.

WORKSHEET 4.2. Tough Transitions and Getting Back on Track

While you complete this worksheet, spend some time thinking about your parenting style, your child's overall mood and temperament, and your home environment. By writing things down and being proactive (instead of reactive) about possible issues, you will be more likely to follow through on the plan that you are setting. Remember, you can always return to an earlier part of the chapter for a refresher on a specific skill.

1. Which tough transition will my child make soon?
   – Crib to bed
   – Nap transitions
   – Eliminating a pacifier
   – Bed-wetting

2. If my child has already made one of these transitions (or not) and is off track, what are my biggest concerns for my child's sleep right now?
   _____
   _____

3. What strategies will I use from this chapter?
   – Sleep hygiene cleanup
   – Parental presence
   – Modified extinction

WORKSHEET 4.2. Tough Transitions and Getting Back on Track (*Continued*)

- — Reduction of liquid in the evening
- — Bed alarms

4. Who will support me in these steps?

_____

_____

5. I would like to complete these steps by this date: _____

(Is there anything that will stop me from starting right away, such as a trip?)

6. My backup plan(s):

_____

_____

What do I think could go wrong? Do I anticipate any pushback from my child or another caregiver? Do I anticipate any barriers that could make it harder for me to follow through with my plan?

_____

_____

If this happens, what can I do? Should I stand strong or pivot? Who can I ask for help?

_____

_____

CHAPTER 5

THINGS THAT GO BUMP IN THE NIGHT: SLEEP TERRORS, SLEEPWALKING, AND NIGHTMARES

Although Chapters 3 and 4 break down sleep difficulties by age, we want to discuss one of the biggest reasons for sleep referrals among children of various ages: parasomnias. *Parasomnias* are undesirable experiences that can occur while we are asleep. Some parasomnias, such as sleep terrors and sleepwalking, occur early in the night during nonrapid-eye-movement (REM) sleep, whereas others, such as nightmares, occur later in the night during REM sleep. It is important to note that all of these parasomnias are entirely out of your child's control and are not behaviorally induced.

Many parasomnias begin or peak at an age that falls between early childhood and the elementary school years. It is important to note that parasomnias can be genetic; if a biological parent experienced them, it is likely that the child may, too. Although most parasomnias are not inherently dangerous or indicative of a larger sleep issue, they can let us know that your child is not getting enough sleep overall; the reason they are not sleeping enough can be behaviorally or medically rooted. As we discussed in Chapter 1, it is important to ensure that your child is not experiencing any symptoms of sleep apnea or restless leg syndrome if they are experiencing parasomnias. Briefly, it is worth consulting a pediatrician if your child snores, gasps, or holds their breath while they sleep or if they complain of itchy or uncomfortable arms and legs while they try to fall asleep. Once we have these medical bases covered, we can get into some behavioral strategies to help with parasomnias.

NONRAPID-EYE-MOVEMENT PARASOMNIAS: SLEEPWALKING, SLEEP TERRORS, AND CONFUSIONAL AROUSALS

When your child *sleepwalks*, they may appear awake and get out of bed to walk around. The average age of sleepwalking onset is between 4 and 6 years. *Sleep terrors* are different. Most parents share that sleep terrors are disturbing and hard to witness: Your child, while still asleep, can scream, cry, and flail and your attempts at soothing are not helpful. The average age of onset for sleep terrors is wider, as they can appear anywhere between ages 4 and 12 years. We refer to them as sleep terrors, rather than night terrors, because they may occur during the day for some very young children that still nap. Finally, *confusional arousals* tend to begin around age 5 and accompany both sleep terrors and sleepwalking. Confusional arousals are similar to sleep terrors, in that children may moan or thrash, but they are milder; they also last longer (on average, about 10–15 minutes).

The first line of treatment for the parasomnias just described is to actually increase your child's overall sleep time, because occurrence can be a sign that your child is sleep deprived. We often see these parasomnias arise when a child is sick or stressed and thus is sleeping less. If your child is younger than 5, revisit Chapter 4 if you need help with behavioral strategies to get your child to sleep more. If your child is age 5 or older, visit Chapter 6 and then return here. Additionally, we recommend taking safety precautions, particularly if your child is getting out of bed and sleepwalking. Specifically, put a bell on your child's door so you know if they are on the move. Also, put baby gates up so your child doesn't attempt to go down any stairs. Fancy toddler door alarms are available that can chirp your cell phone, and home security alarm options that can do the same; jingle bells hanging on a doorknob are also an affordable option. If your child is a frequent sleepwalker, it is also important to ensure that their bedroom floor is free of toys and other debris so they are not at risk of tripping.

We know sleep terrors, confusional arousals, and sleepwalking can be disturbing for parents to witness. Other than ensuring the child's safety and improving their sleep, the best caregiver response to these events is actually to do nothing. We will assume you may have just audibly gasped, because that is what most of our patients' parents do in clinic. We understand that it might be hard for you to heed this advice but please remember, it is better for the child. You can gently guide a sleep-walking child back to bed; however, attempting to rouse or comfort them can prolong the episode or even frighten them if you wake them. Most importantly, children do not remember these episodes in the morning, so you should not remind them of what happened because it may cause them to become anxious and fearful at bedtime. There is no empirical evidence to show that sleep terrors or confusional arousals cause any sort of psychological damage or discomfort, nor do they require comforting or reassurance from parents.

Non–Rapid Eye Movement Parasomnias: The Fast Facts

- Sleepwalking, sleep terrors, and confusional arousals are three common types of non-REM parasomnias, which occur early in the night when deep, slow-wave sleep is most prevalent: These disorders can be genetic; if a biological parent experienced them, the child is more likely to as well.
- Increasing your child's overall amount of sleep can help drastically reduce the occurrence of parasomnias: Other important interventions include introducing safety measures, such

> as door alarms and gates. As hard as it might be, the next best thing to do is nothing. Guide your sleepwalker back to bed gently, but otherwise do not intervene or attempt to rouse them during sleepwalking or sleep terrors.

If you are questioning whether your child is having sleep terrors or nightmares, take the following quiz.

1. When does the episode typically happen?
   a. Early in the night
   b. Late in the night, closer to morning
2. Who remembers the episode?
   a. Just you
   b. Both you and your child
3. How easy is it to wake your child during one of these episodes?
   a. Super hard, because they are basically a zombie
   b. Super easy, and sometimes they are already awake by the time I get to them

If you answered mostly As, your reading is complete: Your child is likely having sleep terrors. If you answered mostly Bs, read on, because your child is likely experiencing nightmares.

NIGHTMARES

Nightmares are sometimes categorized as REM parasomnias, and they are another common source of bedtime anxiety. Nightmares affect a whopping 75% of children (Mindell & Barrett, 2002), with the incidence peaking in middle school. Almost half of children will at some point experience what we call *chronic nightmares*, meaning they occur for more than 6 months at a time. Chronic nightmares can be related to, or caused by, mental health conditions (e.g., anxiety or posttraumatic stress), medication use, or life stress, but they also can occur on their own. Although nightmares are common, we do not want to ignore them or allow them to keep happening to our children, particularly if they are occurring often and causing a significant amount of distress. Unfortunately, we now know that recurrent or distressing nightmares can predict the onset of more serious mental health concerns (Mindell & Barrett, 2002).

We have all been there: We either hear the scream come from our child's room or, even worse, we wake up to their little face 6 inches from our own, saying, "I had a bad dream!" It can be hard to think of what to do when you are half asleep, so we want to equip you with a few behavioral strategies.

Similar to sleep terrors and sleepwalking, nightmares can also be triggered by sleep loss and poor sleep hygiene. Ensure that your little one is getting the sleep they need and has strong sleep habits. If that is squared away and they are still experiencing nightmares, the first thing to do is stay calm and do less overnight when they are upset. Although we might be tempted to ask about the dream or get into a lengthy conversation about dreams not being real, resist the urge! During the night, your only job is to help the child feel safe and secure, then get back to sleep. You can shush them, rub their back, and say something short and sweet (e.g., "You are safe. It was just a dream. Time to sleep").

Sometimes children experience more frequent or distressing dreams or nightmares that linger and upset them when they are awake. Maybe your child complains that the dream keeps popping into their mind or they are afraid to go to sleep for fear that the nightmare might come back. We can address distressing dreams with one of the biggest, as well as the most well researched (St-Onge et al., 2009), tools in our toolbelt: *rescripting* or *image rehearsal therapy*. There are three primary steps:

1. The child writes about (or draws, depending on their age) their upsetting dream. Doing so can be hard and scary for a

child. Feel free to give some snuggles and comfort, reminding your child that they are brave.

2. Help your child pick the main theme of the nightmare, like they would for a story in school. Common main themes of nightmares for children are feeling lost, not knowing where a caregiver is, or feeling unsafe or embarrassed.

3. Finally, here comes the magical part: Your child can change the nightmare any way they wish to reverse this main theme! Tell them that they are the boss of their dreams. They can now rewrite (or redraw) their nightmares and make them happy, secure, or even funny. Completing this process once is powerful; it is even more so if the child rereads the dream a few times during the day and even before bed.

Add a little relaxation before bed, like stretching or deep breathing, and you have a recipe for a restful night!

Nightmares: The Fast Facts

- Nightmares are also triggered by sleep loss, so ensure your little one is getting the appropriate amount of sleep.
- During the night, your only job is to provide comfort to your child and help them get back to sleep. Limit talking.
- If the nightmare feels sticky and distressing, try having your child rescript it when they are awake the next day. Use the following approach:
  - Write or draw the nightmare.
  - Pick the main theme of the nightmare (unsafe, alone, embarrassed) and change it.
  - Write or draw the new dream. Reread the new dream a few times during the day and before bedtime.

Use Worksheet 5.1 to help your child practice rescripting so they can be the boss of their own dreams.

WORKSHEET 5.1. Rescripting—Be the Boss of Your Own Dreams!

Original Nightmare

_____

_____

_____

_____

_____

_____

Main Themes

_____

_____

New Dream

_____

_____

_____

_____

_____

_____

Lena was an 8-year-old girl with recurrent and distressing nightmares. She began to fear and resist bedtime, prompting her parents to seek treatment. She was guided through image rehearsal therapy in session and then later by her parents. In sessions, Lena began with what she decided was her scariest recurrent dream. The original and rescripted dreams are as follows. Note how we try to write them in first person, present tense.

Original Nightmare

I am in my basement playing with my best friend, and we are organizing our Pokémon cards. Suddenly, we hear a noise on the steps that sounds like a big crash. When I look back at my friend, she is gone. Now there is a tall man with a blurry face standing in front of me, trying to grab me. I feel scared and try to run away, but my legs won't work and I can't find the stairs anymore. I try to yell for my friend and then for my parents, and no one hears me. The man keeps getting closer and closer to me. This part feels like it takes forever, and I am terrified. I wake up.

Main Themes

Unsafe, alone

New Dream

I am in the basement playing with my best friend, and we are organizing our Pokémon cards. Suddenly, we hear a noise on the steps that sounds like a big crash. When I look back at my friend, she is gone. Now there is a man with a blurry face standing right in front of me, trying to grab me. I yell for my parents and they come running down into the basement. My dad gives me a hug, and my mom takes off the man's mask: It was a mask! Under the mask I see my teacher who came to surprise me at home! I feel very excited to see him and ask him and my parents to help me organize my cards. I feel safe and happy. I wake up.

CHAPTER 6

DEALING WITH DEFIANCE AND ANXIETY: SLEEP STRATEGIES FOR YOUR BIG KIDS

As children transition into elementary school, their sleep transitions as well. Most notably, they need less sleep (but likely somewhat more than you'd think), they are not napping anymore, and they are more independent in many areas of their lives. Smooth sailing, right?

Along with these exciting transitions come new problems that may arise and catch you off guard. As children enter the elementary school years, they become more aware of the world around them; for some, this can lead to increased anxiety. Also, as they grow more independent and start to develop their sense of self, they may be more defiant and push back around rules and boundaries. Remember, much of this behavior is completely normal and to be expected. In addition to these changes, sleep issues may still be present. For example, your child may attempt to sneak back into your bed after years of sleeping independently, or you are ready to get them to sleep alone if they have not.

Although the strategies you used previously change as your children grow, the foundation you established (with the help of earlier chapters in this book) will still serve you well. In this chapter, we discuss how to get through sleep issues in the elementary years, including targeting sleep anxiety, overcoming behavioral resistance, and getting your big kid to sleep independently.

Finally, each worksheet in this chapter asks you to create a backup plan. Having a backup plan does not mean your original plan won't work: We find that having both in writing can help you follow through and achieve your goals. Kids can be unpredictable, and your best attempts at making significant behavioral changes may not always be perfect because they are *hard*. Our primary goal here is to prevent you from scrapping the plan altogether or backsliding into old habits, such as engaging in power struggles or empty threats. Therefore, it is important to anticipate what may go awry and describe how you will respond.

The first step in tackling difficult sleep in the elementary years is to answer this important question: Where is the sleep issue coming from? To identify the root cause and better address what is happening, we need to determine whether your child's difficulty with sleep is stemming from anxiety or behavioral defiance (or maybe a combination of both).

The key to understanding what will help at night is to look more closely at your child's behavior during the day. Take a few minutes to consider the following questions.

---

1. Does your child often express fears and worries?

   _____

2. Do they have difficulty separating from caregivers in the house during the day?

   _____

3. Does your child typically comply with your directions?

   _____

4. Do they become upset or have a tantrum when they are told "no"?

   _____

---

5. Take a minute to write down five words, a mix of good and bad, that you would use to describe your child. Doing so may also help clarify which direction to go.

_____

_____

6. What do their teachers say about your child and their mood?

_____

_____

_____

_____

If you answered "yes" to question 1 or 2, anxiety may be at the root of your child's bedtime issues. Read the "Bedtime Fears and Anxiety" section of this chapter, and consider whether the plans described fit your situation. If you answered "yes" to question 3 or 4, your child's bedtime issues may have a behavioral root. Read the "Behavioral Defiance as the Cause of Sleep Issues" section of this chapter, and consider whether the plans described fit your situation. Finally, the answers to questions 5 and 6 tell us more about who your child is and how you see them outside of their sleep struggles.

We should also think about how the child behaves when they are struggling with sleep. Do they appear frightened or are they having a tantrum and yelling "no"? Once we have made an educated guess as to the cause, we can pick what to focus on—anxiety or defiance. As you read the plans for each, you may want to pull from both, which can make sense in some cases. Again, nothing is one size fits all, so feel free to pick and choose what works for you and your child.

BEDTIME FEARS AND ANXIETY: THE BRAVE FOUNDATION

When we meet new families in our clinical practices, we rarely make significant sleep changes in the first meeting because it is so important to take time to set a solid foundation of skills. We know it can be frustrating to wait, but you need to get everyone prepared and ready for significant behavioral shifts before making changes. This approach might feel different from other sleep strategies you have used previously. In other programs, the strategies we describe may be used while you are making sleep changes or not at all. We firmly believe it is important to set a strong foundation *before* making sleep changes to increase both your chances of success and your child's feeling of readiness.

If the root of the sleep issues is anxiety, you will focus on establishing the Brave Foundation. Currently, your child probably feels that their best response to being scared is to escape or avoid the stressor. Avoidance can bring initial relief but reinforces the issue in the longer term. Little by little, we want to teach children that they can tolerate those tough feelings and do hard things. Next, we present skills that parents can use to help increase their child's confidence and bravery so they can fight back against their worry when it arises. No matter how brave your child is, it is essential for them to understand that worry may never totally disappear, but they can fight back and not let it derail them. This important skill will serve them well, long beyond their sleep issues.

Skill 1: Brave Bucks

To get your child on board with making changes to their sleep, we need to provide some positive reinforcement across the board. We want you to bulk up the positive attention so your child feels more confident in all aspects of their world, not just with things related to sleep!

The foundation of the Brave Bucks reinforcement system is that children are given one buck each time they exhibit brave behavior during the day. You aim to give positive attention to anything your child does that is challenging or outside their comfort zone (e.g., trying a new food, talking to a new person, or continuing to work on something challenging). Brave Bucks can look however you want; try a token, marble, or coin or use our favorite simple option:

To increase the positive reinforcement of the Brave Buck, add some labeled praises. Fully describe the positive behaviors you are noticing, and tell your child how proud you are of their effort and bravery.

In practice, we hear about a lot of common pitfalls in reward systems, or just generally that they "never work for my kid." Commonly, rewards become stale, they are developmentally inappropriate, or poor management leads to arguments. We recommend you start by creating a reward menu that your child can pick from and trade in some of the bucks they have earned. The menu should have prizes and experiences, like a one-on-one date with you or a special treat. Only give one buck at a time, and never take away bucks as a punishment. Refresh your menu regularly to keep it enticing. Ask your child if there are things they want to put on the menu and work toward.

Skill 2: Having Fun in the Dark

Because so many kids talk about being scared of the dark, having fun in the dark is one specific behavior that always earns a Brave Buck. To decrease your child's fear, plan to do something *not* sleep related, like playing a game, in a dark room. This activity gives your child some exposure to being in the dark and helps them see that the dark does not have to make things scarier. Playing a game can be fun with the lights on, and sometimes it is even more fun to play with the lights off! Flashlight tag and hide-and-seek are great examples of fun games to play.

Skill 3: Worry Time

Worry Time is another strategy that can be used for children with all types of anxiety, not just those with bedtime issues. Rather than your child thinking and talking about worry topics all day long, you provide a set Worry Time each day where they can share their worries with you. Here is how it works:

- Set aside 10 minutes of one-on-one time after dinner and before the bedtime routine begins.
- The child should use that time to talk about all of their worries.
- As the parent, your role can be to listen, help with problem-solving, or both. You know your kid best, so follow their lead.
- If you notice that the same worry thought comes up over and over, you can help your child use facts and logic to challenge it. If your child is scared that someone will break into your home, remind them of the reasons you are less worried about a burglary (e.g., you may have an alarm system or you lock the doors at night).
- If the worry thought continues to return after it has been refuted, have your child label it as a worry thought and tell it

to go away. That is, when a thought becomes "stuck," it is more helpful to teach your child how to say "no" or ignore it rather than continuously argue with it. You can prompt your child to say, "Nope, that is a worry thought. I am going to ignore it!"

Skill 4: Relaxation Strategies (Box Breathing, Progressive Muscle Relaxation, and Guided Imagery)

When we treat children with anxiety, it is invaluable to empower them to feel that they can handle their emotions. Being able to handle emotions does not mean eliminating them; rather, children learn there are things they can do to regulate their body when they are nervous or on edge. Teaching relaxation strategies and helping children recognize what works for them to calm their body can be a simple and effective way to help manage anxiety. We recommend practicing these strategies during calm moments (e.g., maybe on a car ride to a preferred activity), so children can see the impact of these simple strategies on their body even when they are not anxious.

Many activities can be inherently relaxing, such as reading, drawing, or doing mindful meditation. Although all are good options, some of our favorite techniques emphasize actively relaxing the body and focusing on the present (as opposed to the future, which is a common worry among people with anxiety), and they can be done anywhere at any time without additional supplies or materials. These attributes make these techniques easily generalizable to any situation where anxiety may appear, and children learn that they can calm themselves on their own. We describe each next.

The first technique, and one of our personal favorites, is *box breathing*. Taking a deep breath is often a first-line recommendation when we are trying to help someone calm down. Box breathing takes this a step further: Visualize a box as you focus on your breathing (see Figure 6.1). Inhale for 4 seconds (as the first side of the box), hold that breath for 4 seconds (making another side of the

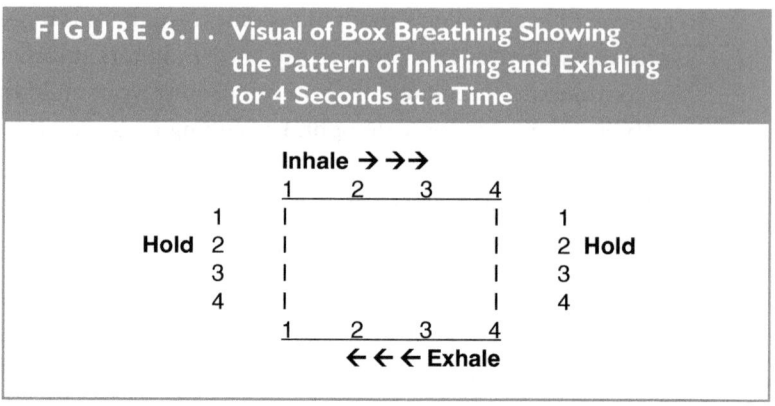

FIGURE 6.1. Visual of Box Breathing Showing the Pattern of Inhaling and Exhaling for 4 Seconds at a Time

box), exhale for 4 seconds (making another side of the box), and then hold your breath again for 4 seconds (closing the box).

Another strategy is *progressive muscle relaxation*, which involves systematically tensing muscle groups and then relaxing them. We typically start at the toes and slowly move upward through the legs, arms, shoulders, and even eyes or ears. While you tense your muscles, take a deep breath and hold it for about 5 seconds. Really take time to notice how your muscles feel. Then take another 5 seconds to relax and exhale, again paying attention to how different relaxation feels. You can do this exercise across your whole body, or you can choose to do just a few muscles; it should only take a few minutes. For children, having something in their hands, such as a pillow or stuffed animal, during this exercise can help them better see the difference between tensing and relaxing their muscles. As they hug the pillow or stuffed animal, they breathe in and squeeze; when they breathe out, they relax their body.

Guided imagery is another technique we use in our clinical practices. Guided imagery is often done initially with someone else leading by asking questions and giving prompts; then it is meant to be done on your own. Throughout the visualization exercise, take slow deep breaths, filling your belly with air, as opposed to more shallow breaths in your chest. First, imagine you are in a place that is truly relaxing and peaceful for you. Then go through each of your senses, really imagining all the things that you will see, smell, touch, and taste—all while focusing on how relaxed you feel when there. For example, if you are thinking about the beach, you may focus on the sound of the waves, the smell of the ocean, the feeling of the sand between your toes, and the overall feeling of calm that you feel when at the beach.

Bedtime Fears and Anxieties: The Fast Facts

- Set the Brave Foundation for 1 to 2 weeks to build your child's confidence in all aspects of their life. The more confident they feel overall, the more open they will be to making sleep changes.
  - Use the Brave Bucks reward system: Give a buck for anything your child does that is brave or out of their comfort zone, sleep related or not! Keep a reward menu so they can cash out some of those bucks for fun prizes or experiences.
  - Try having fun in the dark: One activity that always earns a buck is having fun in the dark. Go play a game in a dark room, and help your child see that the dark does not have to be scary. Rather, it can be fun (and sometimes more fun than being in a bright room)!
- Once you have built up their confidence, you need to show them how to manage and fight back against their worries and fears.
  - Allow Worry Time: Set aside 10 minutes at night, typically after dinner and before the bedtime routine, so your child can have time and space to talk about their worries rather than talking about them all day or at bedtime.

> – Try relaxation strategies: It is important for children to recognize that they can handle their worries and that there are ways that they can calm their body without anything or anyone else. Skills such as box breathing, progressive muscle relaxation, and guided imagery can be helpful to practice when calm so that they can then be used in any stressful situation.

Lena was an 8-year-old girl whose parents described her as having "bedtime anxiety." When her parents were asked what Lena was like during the day, by comparison, they said she was fairly confident and did not seem anxious. However, at bedtime she asked the same questions about burglars and kidnappers over and over again; she often said she was scared to be alone in the dark. Lena's parents built the Brave Foundation by implementing Brave Bucks, having fun in the dark, and using Worry Time. Even with Worry Time, Lena continued to ask questions about burglars and kidnappers at bedtime. Her clinician gave direct directions for her parents to respond with this: "I know you have questions, but Worry Time is over." After a few days of holding their ground, Lena stopped asking this question after the lights went out.

Use Worksheet 6.1 to plan for building the Brave Foundation to help address anxiety.

WORKSHEET 6.1. Building the Brave Foundation

While completing this worksheet, spend some time thinking about your parenting style, your child's overall mood and temperament, and your home environment. By writing things down and being proactive (instead of reactive) about possible issues, you will be more likely to follow through on the plan that you are setting. Remember, you can always return to an earlier part of the chapter for a refresher on a specific skill.

1. How do I think my child's sleep is being impacted by anxiety? What does their anxiety look like at bedtime and overnight? What about during the day?

   _____

   _____

   _____

   _____

2. I will use the following strategies from this chapter:
   - Brave Bucks
   - Having fun in the dark
   - Worry Time

3. Who will support me in these steps?

   _____

   _____

4. I would like to complete these steps by this date: _____

   (Is there anything that will stop me from starting right away, such as a trip?)

5. My backup plan(s):

   _____

   _____

   _____

   _____

6. What do I think could go wrong? Do I anticipate any pushback from my child or another caregiver? Do I anticipate any barriers that could make it harder for me to follow through with my plan?

   _____

   _____

   _____

   _____

   If this happens, what can I do? Should I stand strong or pivot? Who can I ask for help?

   _____

   _____

   _____

   _____

BEHAVIORAL DEFIANCE AS THE CAUSE OF SLEEP ISSUES: SETTING THE STAGE FOR BETTER LISTENING

You have jumped to this section because you decided that your child's difficulties are less about anxiety and more related to behavioral defiance. Although you may want to make significant sleep changes immediately, going slow and steady is more helpful for children who struggle with listening. It is easier to prime them to become better listeners during the day, as opposed to suddenly expecting it at night. Before you make big adjustments to the sleep process, you need to set a foundation for improved compliance and listening. Next, we describe helpful skills for this process.

Skill 1: Behavior Reinforcement via Labeled Praise

During the day, you need to become an ace at noticing your kid being compliant and flexible. Giving *labeled praises* requires you to specifically identify what they did that was helpful and positive. Instead of saying, "Great job!" try this: "Great job being super flexible and letting your sister choose her cookie first!"

Memorize this easy labeled praise: "Thank you for listening the first time I asked." Try to catch the times that your child is compliant, even when doing simple things. Look for flexibility around changes in plans, disappointments, and choices, and offer specific praise (e.g., "I love when you _____," "Thanks for doing _____," or "It's amazing when you _____").

Remember to pick your battles. You don't want to give too much attention to the bad stuff (like when they don't clean up their toys or they leave their shoes in the middle of the kitchen). We always want children to be getting more attention when they are exhibiting helpful and adaptive behaviors than when they are engaging in problematic behavior.

Skill 2: Gotcha Bucks

Your child can earn *Gotcha Bucks* each time they do something flexible or compliant. Gotcha Bucks can look however you want: Try a token, marble, or coin or use our favorite simple option:

In practice, we hear about a lot of common pitfalls in reward systems, or just generally that they "never work for my kid." Commonly, rewards become stale, are developmentally inappropriate, or poor management leads to arguments. We recommend you start by creating a reward menu that your child can pick from and trade in some of the bucks they have earned. The menu should have prizes and experiences, like a one-on-one date with you or a special treat. Only give one buck at a time, and never take away bucks as a punishment. Refresh your menu regularly to keep it enticing. Ask your child if there are things they want to put on the menu and work toward.

Skill 3: One-on-One Time

The concept of *one-on-one time* is loosely borrowed from parent–child interaction therapy (PCIT). PCIT is a protocol of treatment aimed toward improving the defiant or noncompliant behaviors of young children. One-on-one time can be a great tool to increase good listening and mend frayed relationships. Tell your child that this is special one-on-one time for you to play together for a few minutes every day; it is best if you can set a specific time for it so both you and your child know when it is happening. This time is not earned, and it also should never be taken away as a punishment.

Set aside 5 minutes of uninterrupted one-on-one time with your child. The time should be spent engaging in an activity of your child's choosing. Activities like drawing, building with toy bricks, and even playing outside are great. Have your child take the lead, and don't place demands on them or ask a ton of questions. Focus on listening and offering those labeled praises! Praising during play can easily translate to real life, especially with sharing, taking turns, or doing something gently.

Skill 4: Setting a Bedtime Routine With Clear Expectations

The bedtime routine should always be simple, brief, and headed in one direction—bed. Limiting the routine to three to five steps usually works well; always end by saying, "Goodnight!" Here is an example: brush teeth, put on pajamas, read, then goodnight. It is a good idea to make a visual representation of the routine, especially for young kids. Be thoughtful about what you are asking your child to do independently. It can be helpful to temporarily offer them a little more support in the bedtime process, like helping them put on pajamas rather than expecting them to do it alone.

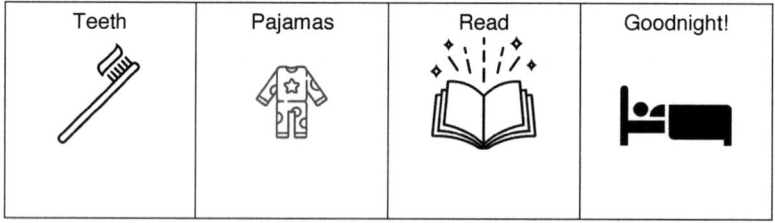

Do you notice that your kid is moving quickly and easily through the bedtime routine? Offer a labeled praise thanking them for working hard or remembering the steps! Try to ignore the small protests and bids for negative attention (e.g., "I'm not tired," or "I don't want to go to sleep"). Many children will ask for food, water, or another bathroom break to stall bedtime. Take time to notice your child's patterns and plan for ways to get ahead of the anticipated callbacks. For example, if your child often requests water, put a bedtime cup in their room that they can easily access. If they request food, offer a "final snack" about 45 minutes before bed and set the stage for no more snacks after that. The need for the bathroom can be a bit more challenging: Ensure that your child always goes to the bathroom before they get into bed, and encourage them to use the bathroom independently if they need to go again. We recommend that you trust your gut and what your child truly does and does not need. Remember, kids quickly notice patterns: If you say yes to a snack on Monday, don't be surprised if they ask for a snack again on Tuesday!

Ultimately, it is important to remember that building a strong relationship with your child, filled with loads of positive attention, can improve their listening skills around sleep *and* other behaviors. Having your child listen and follow directions is key for successful sleep, because you want them to know what you expect of them and what your response will be. Through attention, praise, and consistency, you will set a strong foundation for better sleep.

Behavioral Defiance: The Fast Facts

- To set a foundation for better listening and flexibility, we need to start with lots of positive attention and reinforcement: Positive attention and reinforcement are for all

things, not just those related to sleep, so that your child feels more ready to change their sleep.
- Try the labeled praise and Gotcha Bucks reward systems: Give clear and specific praise any time you see your child being compliant and flexible ("Thank you for _____" is a great place to start). Give a buck for good listening or flexibility, and keep a reward menu that your child can use to cash out those bucks for something fun or special.
- Offer one-on-one time: Set aside 5 minutes of uninterrupted one-on-one time with your child. Focus on following their lead without asking questions or giving commands, and give lots of labeled praise to show you are engaged and enjoying the time together.
- Follow a quick and simple bedtime routine: The best bedtime routine is simple with no more than three to five steps. It should always end with "Goodnight!"
- Back up, but don't back down: You can make a small shift to your plan (e.g., decreasing a check-in interval from 5 minutes to 3 minutes) without totally caving or giving in.

Nik was a 6-year-old boy who presented to treatment with a lot of energy. He struggled to listen to his parents at home and fought bedtime. At first, his parents were coached to work on ignoring some of his smaller behaviors, such as whining. They used labeled praise and Gotcha Bucks when he was flexible and did well with listening to small requests. They also began alternating days for one-on-one time with him, which he loved. Finally, they were coached to make their bedtime routine shorter and easier. Prior to treatment, they were spending an hour going through their bedtime activities and also chasing Nik and trying to corral him. In session, they created a visual schedule that was more streamlined and included potty, teeth, pajamas, and reading comics (something Nik loved to do and was previously doing at the beginning of their routine). Nik's parents learned to stop paying so much attention to his small bids for attention, such as when he tried to insist that he wasn't tired. They got better at praising him for when he was moving quickly, reminding him that he was getting closer to earning his morning reward for successfully completing the routine each day.

Use Worksheet 6.2 to create a plan to improve your child's listening, with the aim to also improve their sleep.

WORKSHEET 6.2. Setting the Stage for Better Listening

While you complete this worksheet, spend some time thinking about your parenting style, your child's overall mood and temperament, and your home environment. By writing things down and being proactive (instead of reactive) about possible issues, you will be more likely to follow through on the plan that you are setting. Remember, you can always return to an earlier part of the chapter for a refresher on a specific skill.

1. How do I think behavioral defiance is impacting my child's sleep? What does their defiance look like at bedtime and overnight? What about during the day?

   _____

   _____

   _____

   _____

2. I will use the following strategies from this chapter:
   - Labeled praise
   - Gotcha Bucks
   - One-on-one time
   - Create a bedtime routine

(continues)

WORKSHEET 6.2. Setting the Stage for Better Listening (*Continued*)

3. Who will support me in these steps?

   _____

   _____

4. I would like to complete these steps by this date: _____

   (Is there anything that will stop me from starting right away, such as a trip?)

5. My backup plan(s):

   _____

   _____

6. What do I think could go wrong? Do I anticipate any pushback from my child or another caregiver? Do I anticipate any barriers that could make it harder for me to follow through with my plan?

   _____

   _____

   _____

   _____

   If this happens, what can I do? Should I stand strong or pivot? Who can I ask for help?

   _____

   _____

   _____

   _____

WITH THE FOUNDATION SET, LET'S GET YOUR CHILD TO FALL ASLEEP MORE INDEPENDENTLY

Now that the foundation is set, whether it be for bravery or better listening, we are ready to tackle the bedtime battle. Perhaps your child requires someone with them to fall asleep, sleeps in your bed, or comes out of their room multiple times after the bedtime routine is complete (we call this the *curtain call*). Next, we present strategies you can use to help your child sleep independently, regardless of whether the root of the sleep issue is anxiety or behavioral defiance (or both).

Skill 1: Bedtime Pass

Bedtime passes can be used to cut back on curtain calls regardless of the root of the sleep issue. Here is how they work:

- Pick a set number of passes and put them on your child's door: The passes can be simple sticky notes, or some kids like to make their own passes. We often start with three passes, but you may need a few more if your child is leaving the room more than five or six times per night. Another option is to keep the passes on your child's nightstand so they are right in front of them (hopefully prompting them to think, "Do I want to use this pass or not?"). We use both approaches and encourage you to think about what might work best for your family. You can even talk to your child about their preference.
- Each time your child leaves the room, you take a pass from the door or nightstand.
- When there are no sticky notes left, your child should not leave the room. If they do, walk them back to the room without any chitchat or explanation.
- In the morning, trade the remaining sticky notes for Gotcha or Brave Bucks. A one-to-one exchange rate is recommended.
- Slowly cut back the number of sticky notes on the door, but know that some people keep one on the door for a long time. It can be comforting and it works, so no need to change something that helps!

Skill 2: Bedtime Check-In

With *bedtime check-ins*, you say goodnight to your child at bedtime and then periodically come back to check on them at set intervals, which increase each night. For example, night 1 is 2-minute intervals, night 2 is 4-minute intervals, night 3 is 6-minute intervals, and so on. With super anxious kids who jump out of bed, we would start with even smaller intervals. That first night, the checks might be just 1 minute apart, bumping up by a single minute each night. Here are some tips:

- Checks should be brief pop-ins with *very* minimal interaction, if any at all.
- The checks can only happen if the child remains in bed.
- If your child gets out of bed, calmly remind them that you cannot reenter their room for a check until they are back in bed.
- Offer a Gotcha Buck and a labeled praise in the morning if they stay in bed.
- Ignore any whining or chatting, as long as your child stays in bed.
- You are "done" when your child is consistently falling asleep during that first check.

Skill 3: Camping Out (Parental Presence)

Camping out is what the name suggests: You say goodnight and stay (camp out) in your child's room until they fall asleep. Here is how it works:

- Typically, you sit on a chair or on the floor, as opposed to sitting on your child's bed. Make a clear schedule that transitions every

2 to 3 days and start small. If your child is currently sleeping in your room, your first step would place you physically in the bed with them until they fall asleep. If you are currently in the bed with them while they fall asleep, your first step is just sitting up in the bed.

- Every 2 to 3 days, start shifting out of the room. For example, start next to the bed, then move halfway across the room, to the doorway, and right outside the door.
- Your child will earn a Gotcha Buck the next morning if they stay in bed during the night. If they get up to use the bathroom, they can still earn a Gotcha Buck; the goal is for them to use the bathroom independently and without intentionally waking anyone else.

Skill 4: The Break Method

Before you start the *break method*, track your child's sleep for 1 week. To determine the average amount of time it takes your child to fall asleep (*sleep latency*), make note of (a) when they went to bed and (b) when they actually fell asleep. It can be helpful to have a baby monitor in the room to see when your child falls asleep. For this example, assume it takes 20 minutes for your child to fall asleep from the time they go to bed. Now you are ready to begin the break method.

- Once you have said goodnight to your child, stay with them for half of their sleep latency period. In this case, that would be 10 minutes. At the 10-minute mark, take a 1-minute break outside the room and then return, staying until your child is asleep. It is not necessary to say anything when you leave, but you can tell them quickly that you will be right back. This process should be explained and even rehearsed during the day before you start, so they will know what is happening.

- Each night, extend the break by 1 additional minute until your child is falling asleep alone each night. Afterward, you can either begin to reduce those first 10 minutes in their room at the beginning or leave them in place.
- Your child will earn a Gotcha Buck or Brave Buck the next morning if they stay in bed during this process.

After you select a method and talk it out with your child, which we highly recommend, it is important to ensure everyone is on board and on the same page. Another step we strongly recommend is *daytime rehearsal*. If we opt to use the break method or check-ins, it can be helpful for children to know how long these breaks feel. Flex your acting muscles and pretend to settle them into bed and rehearse the process. Adding big praise and a Gotcha Buck or Brave Buck will help prime them well.

BEDTIME FADING

People often ask how long it should take for a child to fall asleep. Generally, we view 30 minutes or less as an appropriate amount of time. Occasionally, even when a child still has a parent with them as they fall asleep, they take longer than 30 minutes to fall asleep: This may indicate that their bedtime is too early or that their body clock may be a little out of sync with their bedtime. When this happens, try *bedtime fading*. To do this, take 1 week to track what time your child actually falls asleep. For example, the child's bedtime is 8:30 p.m., but they typically do not fall asleep until 9:30 p.m. Temporarily start putting them to bed closer to their true fall-asleep time. Once you observe your child falling asleep faster, in consistently less than

30 minutes, start shifting their bedtime back 15 minutes per night until the desired time is reached.

Struggles With Falling Asleep and Staying Asleep

What do we do about sleep struggles in the middle of the night? It can be overwhelming if your child has problems with falling asleep *and* staying asleep. We get it! Make it more manageable for everyone involved and start by tackling only bedtime first. Doing so means you are more functional and awake, and therefore more likely to be consistent with your plan. For example, if prior to making sleep changes you go into your child's room to console them when they wake, keep doing this for now.

When you feel like bedtime has gotten better and your nights are feeling calmer and more successful, take a minute to think about what worked and what got you there. Then apply the same tools to any middle-of-the-night sleep issues. If bedtime passes worked best at bedtime, get those sticky notes out again and lay out the expectations and rewards for what the middle of the night will look like. The good news is that because we have spent so much time setting a foundation and building confidence with independent sleep at bedtime, this last step tends to move quickly and easily.

Backup Plans

Even the best laid plans can go off course, so what do you do when things go awry? You look at your backup plans! In Worksheets 6.1 to 6.3, you set backup plans to help you address your child's sleep issues.

Let's say that, after doing your prep work, you take a step and it does not go as planned. You might experience what we call the extinction burst. An *extinction burst* is a burst of negative behavior in response to the change you made. It might look like screaming,

crying, or just general resistance. If you find yourself in this situation, all hope is not lost, and you have a few options:

1. *You can remain firm and wait out the extinction burst.* If you
   hold steady with your plan, your child should respond and
   eventually fall in line after a few days. Don't move forward to
   the next step of the plan until the extinction burst ends.
2. *Back up without backing down.* You can take a very small
   step back, without totally caving. For example, if your child
   really struggles with your move to right outside the door, can
   you readjust to be halfway visible in the doorway for a couple
   of days before trying again? If so, give that a try. Don't be too
   reactive with these adjustments though; use them sparingly.

Independent Sleep: The Fast Facts
- Once we have set the foundation, we can work on get-
  ting our kids to sleep independently using the following:
  - Bedtime passes
  - Bedtime check-ins
  - Camping out
- Rehearsing your chosen method during the daytime can
  help ease the first night tremendously.
- If your child is also having difficulty in the middle of
  the night, focus on bedtime first and then take whatever
  strategies worked then and apply them to the middle-of-
  the-night wakings.
- If things don't go as planned and your child seems to be
  struggling more than you anticipated, you have two options:
  - Wait it out: Remain firm with your choices and your
    plan, and see if your child can adjust with time.

> – Back up, but don't back down: Take a small step back in your plan and hold steady for a bit before moving forward.

Lena's parents used bedtime passes because she usually came out of her room at bedtime and overnight. Lena usually came out of her room three to four times at bedtime, so they started with three passes on her door at bedtime. They removed one pass after 3 days of "success," which was defined as only using two passes, rather than all three. Unfortunately, Lena did get stuck at two passes for quite some time. Her parents felt discouraged, like they might never get her to sleep alone, as it seemed she was always using both passes and not bothering to save any until the morning. They debated just holding steady, but ultimately decided to revisit her reward menu associated with her reward system. Lena was able to identify a highly desirable reward that relit the fire underneath her to move forward. Finally, Lena was still coming out of her room to get her parents about two times per night at this point, so they decided to give her just one overnight pass. She used that one pass for an entire week before she stopped coming out of her room overnight.

Fortunately for Nik's parents, although he struggled to cooperate during the bedtime routine and to stay in bed at bedtime, he was out for the night once he actually fell asleep. To get Nik to stay in bed at bedtime, they began using checks. Because he was so likely to get up before falling asleep, they started with very small checks at just 30 seconds. The idea was that they would come back quickly so he did not have the chance to get out of bed. They then increased the time of the checks: 1-minute intervals, then 2-minute intervals, and so on. Because Nik had such early success with the quick checks, he did well with making the checks longer and began falling asleep when they reached 15 minutes apart.

Complete Worksheet 6.3 to set a plan for helping your child achieve independent sleep.

WORKSHEET 6.3. Independent Sleep

While you complete this worksheet, spend some time thinking about your parenting style, your child's overall mood and temperament, and your home environment. By writing things down and being proactive (instead of reactive) about possible issues, you will be more likely to follow through on the plan that you are setting. Remember, you can always return to an earlier part of the chapter for a refresher on a specific skill.

1. I will use the following strategies from this chapter:
   – Bedtime passes
   – Checks
   – Parental presence
   – Break method
   – Bedtime fading
   – Middle-of-the-night follow-up

2. Who will support me in these steps?
   _____
   _____

3. I would like to complete these steps by this date: _____

   (Is there anything that will stop me from starting right away, such as a trip?)

4. It is important for the family to be on the same page when implementing a new plan like this. How and when will I discuss this with my child and sleep team members?
   _____
   _____

5. My backup plan(s):
   _____
   _____

WORKSHEET 6.3. Independent Sleep (*Continued*)

6. What do I think could go wrong? Do I anticipate any pushback from my child or another caregiver? Do I anticipate any barriers that could make it harder for me to follow through with my plan?

_____

_____

_____

_____

If this happens, what can I do? Should I stand strong or pivot? Who can I ask for help?

_____

_____

_____

_____

CHAPTER 7

ALMOST A TEENAGER: GET READY!

Adolescent sleep requires a different approach that largely focuses on the teen rather than their caregiver. Although adolescent sleep is not a focus of this book, we don't want to leave you hanging: In this chapter, we share ways to manage certain sleep difficulties that arise in the adolescent years, with a focus on improving understanding of the normal shift that occurs over time. We also provide strategies to set your household up for success as your child gets older.

BECOMING A NIGHT OWL AND DETERMINING HOW MUCH SLEEP TEENS REALLY NEED

To the surprise of many, teens should still sleep between 8 to 10 hours per night (Moore & Meltzer, 2008). This recommendation is backed not only by research but also by the American Academy of Sleep Medicine (2016) and the U.S. Centers for Disease Control and Prevention (2020), among others. We know this may raise some eyebrows or have you muttering, "Yeah, right!" because you may not know many teenagers who get 8 hours of sleep most nights. There are a few well-known reasons why adolescents do not get enough sleep, such as early school start times, extracurricular expectations (including sports or an after-school job), and use of cell phones and other electronics. Across a person's lifetime, the preferred sleep schedule tends to begin and end early, especially in infancy and again in older age. However, youths experience a biological shift to evening-ness in adolescence, or put simply, they become "night owls" (Hagenauer et al., 2009). For example, a preteen who used to easily fall asleep around 10:00 p.m. may suddenly struggle to fall asleep until mid-night or 1:00 a.m. Waking them for school may become difficult because their morning waking preferences shift as well.

Apart from sleep shifts, what other sleep issues can we expect during adolescence? Having a teenager at home can feel chaotic. One of the most common caregiver questions we get in clinical practice is, "Is this normal?" Regardless of the behavior, we often consider whether it is interfering with the teen's daily functioning, school-work, social life, and possibly work. In terms of sleep, how do we identify a typical shift in teen sleep versus a clinically concerning one? Here is the short answer: When the shift interferes with their daily functioning at school, socializing, or work, it becomes a concern. The long answer is more complex.

In the United States, most high schools start early in the morning (i.e., 8:00 a.m. or earlier, as discussed later in this chapter). Coupled with late extracurricular schedules and social commitments, it is no surprise that teens may feel perpetually exhausted. As clinicians, we become concerned when teens present symptoms of excessive day-time sleepiness. In clinic, *multiple sleep latency tests* (or nap tests) are conducted to examine daytime sleepiness. If teens are offered the opportunity to nap at varying times across the day, we can gauge their daytime sleepiness by seeing whether they fall asleep and, if so, how quickly. If your teen or preteen is falling asleep consistently in classes or at other times during the day, this may be a reason for concern. As for biologically becoming a night owl, it is reasonable for older children to stay up later and sleep in during the week-end. However, if they are sleeping in several hours or consistently struggling to fall asleep (or both) on weekdays, this is another reason for concern.

It is also important to discern typical teen and preteen sleepiness from other symptoms or sleepiness associated with a mental health condition. Most, if not all, mental health conditions have symptoms that affect sleep. For example, when sleep loss is associated with anxiety or depression in adolescents, it can actually worsen the mental health condition. Increased fatigue can contribute to social isolation in adolescent depression as well. Research has shown that sleep loss can be associated with more high-risk behavior in adolescents, such as self-harm and substance use, both of which are linked to mental health struggles. It is important to be extra watchful and seek clinical intervention when sleep changes are believed to be associated with a mental health condition. On a more hopeful note, addressing symptoms of sleep loss in any of these conditions can help with symptom relief. Finally, if your teen or preteen is consistently getting the recommended amount of sleep and continues to feel like they are not well rested, they should be medically evaluated.

Becoming a Night Owl and What Is Normal: The Fast Facts

- It is normal to expect teens and preteens to experience more sleepiness, but we should be concerned if they do any of the following:
  - display symptoms of excessive daytime sleepiness, such as frequent, accidental naps;
  - struggle to fall asleep on weekdays and wake on weekends;
  - experience significant sleep changes associated with a confirmed or suspected mental health condition; or
  - are getting the recommended amount of sleep but consistently still do not feel rested.

Lena was a 13-year-old girl who presented for therapy to address symptoms of depression and anxiety, as well as associated school refusal behavior. She also struggled with what she labeled as insomnia, in that she felt she did not sleep enough and was often exhausted during the day. After 9 months of treatment with a cognitive behavioral therapist, her symptoms of anxiety and depression significantly improved, but Lena still felt she was not sleeping well and struggled to attend school 3 to 4 days per week. At this point, Lena's primary therapist referred her for behavioral sleep treatment.

Is It Actually Insomnia? Common Sleep Diagnoses in Adolescence

The term *insomnia* is used loosely these days to describe myriad sleep difficulties, including recurrent night wakings, nonrestorative sleep, and even just one tough night. Clinical insomnia is defined by difficulty falling asleep, staying asleep, or waking earlier in the morning than desired, occurring at least 3 nights out of the week and lasting for at least 3 months. Additionally, when we diagnose insomnia, we ensure it is not better explained by a different sleep–wake disorder, such as delayed sleep phase disorder. A *phase delay* means the entire sleep schedule shifts forward at least 2 hours: For example, your child previously fell asleep at 10:00 p.m. and woke at 6:00 a.m. for school, and now they are unable to fall asleep until 12:00 a.m. and do not wake until 8:00 a.m. Individuals with insomnia typically struggle to fall asleep any time they try; those with delayed sleep phase disorder can fall asleep faster when they attempt to sleep at a later time aligned with their circadian rhythms.

It is important to note that some adolescents do not meet full criteria for either diagnosis but are still troubled by something nonclinical called *social jet lag*. In typical posttravel jet lag, a person's body is dragged across time zones. In the case of social jet lag, we feel like our body has been dragged across time zones but no fun travel goes with it. Primarily in high school, teens are expected to begin school very early, necessitating an early bedtime, and then they stay out and sleep in later due to either their night owl nature or social obligations. Can you imagine flying from New York to California every Monday and then back again on Friday? Even if you did that, you would be in better shape because you would have the sun to help reset your internal body clock, or circadian rhythms. With social jet lag, there are no natural cues that help reset the teen's body. Social jet lag is not just being tired all the time; it is literally changing "time zones" between the weekdays and weekends (and in turn, shifting the schedule by several hours.)

Insomnia and Other Diagnoses: The Fast Facts

- There are a few common sleep disorders we see in adolescents:
  - Insomnia is difficulty falling asleep, staying asleep, or waking too early.
  - Delayed sleep phase occurs when the sleep schedule shifts forward at least 2 hours for both sleep and wake times.
- Many teens experience social jet lag due to the demands of their school and social schedules (much like being in one time zone during the week and in another on the weekends).

BE PREPARED: TIPS TO HELP ADOLESCENT SLEEP

Being equipped with a few tips to help with adolescent sleep struggles may make them seem less challenging. First, always start by updating a few basic sleep hygiene practices. The same rules apply here as they did in childhood—rooms should be kept cool, dark, and quiet. Your teen should have a simple bedtime routine and avoid caffeine, heavy meals, and large amounts of liquid right before bed. The recommendations to only use the bed for sleep and to maintain a consistent schedule hold true, although they are more complicated at this age. As we mentioned earlier in this chapter, wanting more alone time in adolescence is not a reason for concern. It is developmentally typical for children to look for autonomy and time to themselves at this age. When it comes to their sleep, the problem is when teens seek that autonomy in their room—mainly in their bed, doing anything but sleeping. For example, they are on their phone, playing video games, and talking to friends while in bed. Spending many waking hours in bed creates a negative cycle. The brain and the body rely on cues when it is time to sleep, and getting into bed is one of the biggest cues. So, we do not want to confuse those signals by hanging out a lot in bed. Providing an additional, comfortable seating space in your adolescent's room can be a simple way to avoid this bad habit. If this is not possible or space is tight, help them find another comfortable spot in your home where they can have some periodic alone time.

Because it is difficult for teens to maintain a consistent sleep-wake schedule, it is important to be a bit more flexible when it will not be possible for them to get enough sleep during the week. We suggest allowing for an extra hour of sleep on the weekends, as this can be okay for some teens and does not interfere with their ability to fall asleep earlier during the week. If you see this hour negatively impacting them, try shortening it a bit. Additionally, there are other, more proactive practices we can use to aid against social jet lag, promote a more consistent sleep–wake schedule, and help the teen feel more well rested. Examples include getting out of bed and getting exposure to natural light in the morning hours. Help your adolescent create a morning routine that makes it more enticing to get out of bed, rather than snooze or lie there for a prolonged period of time. Additionally, we want to stick with limiting caffeine and exercise in the late afternoon and evening hours and even using well-timed naps. Yes, naps! Again, if you find that it does not interfere with bedtime, a brief 30-minute nap immediately after school can be extremely helpful for sleepy teens.

As we mentioned, getting bright light in the morning hours can help teens, and everyone, sleep better. How about limiting light in the evening? Screen use and its negative impact on sleep becomes much more troublesome in the adolescent years. Screens are a way of life, between schoolwork, gaming, and socializing. The biggest piece of advice we can give about screens is to have a clear and consistent policy around screen use, particularly in the evening. Bolster this policy by setting an example and making it family-wide. For example, charge your cell phone in the kitchen instead of the bedroom. Our other piece of advice is to be realistic. Attempting to ban all screens in the hours before bedtime likely will not work. Instead, focus on the type of screen and the content. Games and content that are more cognitively arousing, or get our brains and emotions charged, are more disruptive to sleep. Logically, a tablet or phone held inches from our face is more disruptive than a television screen several feet away in a dimly lit room.

Earlier in this book, we described a healthy example we set for infants, and this applies to teens as well: Prioritize sleep! Although caregivers and adolescents often feel they have a never-ending list of tasks to complete in 24 hours, prioritizing sleep is important for all ages (visit Chapter 3 for a refresher). When you're tackling a pile of things to do once everyone else has gone to bed, ask yourself: What must be done before tomorrow? What would I like to get done for tomorrow? What can wait until tomorrow (or later)? And what do others want me to get done for tomorrow? If the answer is not obvious, skip the task and go to sleep.

Finally, get involved! We would be remiss if we did not use this chapter to educate parents on the detrimental effects of early school start times on teens. Due to concerns around busing and athletics, the average U.S. public high school begins at 8:00 a.m. or earlier (Sawyer & Taie, 2020). In 2014, the American Academy of Pediatrics issued a statement recommending that high school start times be changed to no earlier than 8:30 a.m. (Adolescent Sleep Working Group, 2014). This position has been echoed by many reputable organizations since then, including the American Medical Association (2016) and the American Academy of Sleep Medicine (Watson et al., 2017). We know unquestionably that U.S. teens are at greater risk for sleep loss, with myriad potential associated risk factors including increased mental health and physical health risks. One particularly salient risk for this age group, which is often missed, is the impact of sleep deprivation on driving. Research has shown us time and again that the incidence of car crashes increases exponentially when drivers are sleep deprived (Sprajcer et al., 2023). In a previous study, Bin-Hasan et al. (2020) found that a decrease in teen car crashes was correlated with later school start times. If you want to get involved and make meaningful changes for your child and others, we advise that you speak with your school board members about start times or join a reputable organization such as Start School Later, which is already years into fighting this battle.

Tips to Get Ahead of Tired Teens: The Fast Facts

- Encourage your teen to maintain good sleep hygiene patterns from childhood: Their bedroom should be cool, dark, and quiet. They should avoid caffeine, rigorous exercise, large meals, and large amounts of liquid in the hour before bed.
- Create some new, healthy sleep habits: Establish a comfortable seating space in your preteen's room to avoid them hanging out in bed while awake. Create a morning routine to help encourage your preteen to get out of bed.

Prioritize sleep for yourself and your preteen: Ask yourself what really needs to get done before bed.

- Here's the skinny on screens and preteens: Leading by example and having the whole family shut down to prepare for bed is helpful. Focus mostly on the content and type of screen, rather than a full ban on screens. In the ideal world, we are not exposed to screens in the hour before bed.
- Another opportunity to lead by example is showing teens how to prioritize sleep: Teens are at an age where they are inundated with schoolwork, extracurricular activities, and social responsibilities. This is a good age to start learning how to prioritize and decide what can wait until tomorrow.
- Get involved! Make a change that reaches beyond just your teen and fight back against early school start times by joining an organization like Start School Later.

SLEEP INERTIA

Why is it so hard for teens to get out of bed in the morning? *Sleep inertia* is simply that feeling of grogginess or heaviness upon waking, and it tends to impact teens more than any other age demographic. This feeling tends to cause them to want to stay in bed or go back to sleep. It typically abates after about a half hour, but in some cases, it can last a few hours. Sleep inertia can be further complicated by anxiety and depression, in that staying in bed feeds into depression-related fatigue and anxious avoidance of starting one's day. A few things that help teens with sleep inertia are as follows:

- Attempt to keep a more consistent sleep schedule.
- Get natural light, or light from a therapy light box, soon after waking.

- Have a caffeinated beverage soon after waking.
- Take a cold shower soon after waking.

After determining that Lena met criteria for delayed sleep–wake phase disorder, and not insomnia, some small strategies were implemented to help improve her sleep. Some of these strategies were a direct intervention for Lena (not important to mention here), and some were directed toward Lena's caregiver, her father. Lena's household was a very busy one, particularly for her father, who was a single parent. He reported that he typically worked late into the evening in his office, but then continued to work from home into the early hours of the morning most days. While her father worked at home, Lena typically kept busy gaming. Her late naps and evening caffeine consumption effectively existed to service her ability to stay awake and game. Once Lena's father understood how her school refusal behavior was strongly tied to her sleep behavior, he felt more on board with making changes and adding more structure in the household. In a meeting with both Lena and her father, it was agreed that evening caffeine and napping would stop, with the support of and mostly increased oversight from her father. He bought her a hanging chair for her room so that when she did game or read, she could do it outside of bed. Finally, and possibly most importantly, Lena and her father started mutually unplugging at 10:00 p.m., which was not the most ideal time but a good compromise for all.

With some more individual sleep strategies implemented, in conjunction with support around anxiety, depression, and school refusal from her primary therapist, after about 4 weeks Lena was eventually able to get on a sleep schedule that allowed her to feel consistently more well rested. Everyone observed an additional improvement in symptoms of anxiety, depression, and increased school attendance.

Complete Worksheet 7.1 to help prepare for your child's sleep in the teen years.

WORKSHEET 7.1. Prepping for the Teen Years

While you complete this worksheet, spend some time thinking about your parenting style, your child's overall mood and temperament, and your home environment. By writing things down and being proactive (instead of reactive) about possible issues, you will be more likely to follow through on the plan that you are setting. Remember, you can always return to an earlier part of the chapter for a refresher on a specific skill.

1. What sleep changes am I most fearful of in my child's teen years?
   - Not getting enough sleep due to schedule restrictions
   - Sleep changes associated with puberty and biological shifts
   - Sleep changes associated with mental health concerns
   - Screen use interfering with sleep
   - Drowsy driving

   Take a moment to write down what current behavior(s) supports your predictions for the teen concerns you just checked:

   _____

   _____

   _____

   _____

2. What strategies do I particularly want to use as my child ages into their teen years?
   - Clean up basic sleep hygiene
   - Create a seating space in my child's room
   - Help them to maintain a consistent sleep schedule
   - Have consistent expectations and schedules around screen use
   - Help them learn to prioritize sleep along with additional responsibilities and tasks
   - Create a morning routine to help my child get out of bed
   - Lead by example!
   - Get involved with an organization like Start School Later

(*continues*)

WORKSHEET 7.1. Prepping for the Teen Years
(Continued)

3. Who will support me in these steps?

   _____

   _____

4. My backup plan(s):

   _____

   _____

   _____

   _____

   What do I think could go wrong? Do I anticipate any barriers that could make it harder for me to follow through with my plan?

   _____

   _____

   _____

   _____

   If this happens, what can I do? Should I keep moving forward or pause training? Who can I ask for help?

   _____

   _____

   _____

   _____

CHAPTER 8

WRAPPING UP AND TROUBLESHOOTING

At this point, we hope that everyone in your home is sleeping through the night and you feel more confident in your success. In this chapter, we discuss how to maintain this progress and overcome some likely inevitable bumps in the road: both expected and unexpected. So often in our clinical work, families come in telling us that all was good until their child got sick or the whole family slept in one room on a week-long vacation. Understandably, these types of events should shift systems and expectations for sleep, but they do not need to completely derail them. As you have done before in this workbook, take some time to reflect: This time, think about your successes and what has gotten you this far.

Take a moment to write about how things feel different in your home now that sleep has improved:

_____

_____

_____

_____

(continues)

Now, please write about why you would like to maintain this progress:

_____

_____

_____

_____

CHANGES TO EXPECT

As children age, you can expect certain changes in both their sleep needs and their temperament and behavior. We are commonly asked, "How much sleep does my child need per day?" Here are some general ranges:

Age	Total hours of sleep
Infancy	12–15 (including naps)
Toddler and preschool age	11–14 (including naps)
Elementary and middle school age	9–11
Teen	8–10

As shown in these ranges and described earlier in this book, infants require the most sleep (both naps and overnight). As they become toddlers and preschoolers, they begin to sleep a little less, and we expect the "terrible twos" and increased defiance. These behavior changes stem from a normative developmental urge to push back on boundaries. As children enter their school years, their overall needed amount of sleep further decreases; their need to push back also may decrease, but their desire for independence will likely increase.

The need for independence emerges strongly in the teen years. Although this book does not directly address sleep in adolescence, we share a few thoughts on this transition to set you up for success. As we mentioned in Chapter 7, teens typically are night owls, saddled with early school start times and tons of evening activities. Continue encouraging your teen to prioritize a good night's sleep, and help them organize their evening routine to allow for a rational bedtime. Clinically speaking, it is not abnormal for teens to want to spend time alone in their room each day, within reason. However, for the sake of sleep hygiene, your teen should *not* spend all of this time in their bed. Remember our message from Chapter 1: Bed is for sleep. One simple, small task you can accomplish right now to help your future teen's sleep is to ensure they have somewhere cozy to sit in their room that is not their bed: Ensure they are not reading, gaming, or doing homework all day in bed by providing them this alternative space.

CHANGES THAT ARE LESS EXPECTED

Things will occur in life that may derail your sleep progress. Vacations, illness, and the beginning and end of Daylight Saving Time are a few common examples. We often tell families that although we are happy to see them again after they complete treatment the first time, we want them to feel confident to independently regain control after they hit one of these bumps in the road. Regaining control begins with the power of our words. Even at a young age, children can start to appreciate language that clearly categorizes a behavior when used sparingly. Here are some examples that indicate a clear deviation from the norm: "We are all sleeping in one room because we are on vacation," or "You are sleeping with us because you are sick." We can use the following examples to remind children of our expectations of them: "We are home, so you sleep in your room," or "You are feeling better, so I will not be coming into your room tonight."

Of course, it is not always so simple. Children may not take us seriously or they may laugh in our faces when we use these phrases to regain control. Should this happen, do not panic! You have righted the ship before (we assume with the help of this book), and you can do it again by leaning on the strategies you found successful. For example, if you took timed breaks out of the room at bedtime in the beginning, do it again now but maybe just move a bit faster. That is, rather than increasing the break by 1 minute each night, increase it by 2 minutes or 5 minutes if you feel your child can tolerate it. It can also be helpful to bring back those reward systems you've used—but temporarily. Make it abundantly clear to your child that, as the parent or caregiver, you still have the same expectations for your child's sleep behavior, and the goal will be to meet these expectations. These same rules apply for our least favorite type of unexpected change—the one caused by literally nothing. Kids are ever-changing, growing, and developing. Weird things are bound to happen. Expect them to have little backslides and hiccups now and again. We actually recommend that you try watchful waiting when this first occurs. Maybe give your child a week to see whether this really is a new pattern or if it is just a blip. Sometimes they may shock you and go back to their typical behavior within days. Do not stay awake for days on end trying to understand why; just use those old strategies to get your child back on track if they do not do so on their own.

We want to share a quick note on Daylight Saving Time. There are two options we recommend, like most other sleep specialists. You can take this slow and steady by shifting your child's schedule (sleep, meals, and so forth, as much as you can) by 15 minutes each night leading up to the time change. Or you can do nothing. Be reactive to the time change: Get your child on the new clock right away, and remember that it takes people about a week to fully adjust. (Truly, our hope is that by the time this book is published, we have done away with Daylight Saving Time altogether!)

WHEN IS IT TIME TO SEE A SPECIALIST?

As helpful as this book is intended to be, there are certain situations where it may be better for you to speak with a specialist. For example, if your child has autism spectrum disorder or other developmental delays, we recommend you talk with a specialist because sleep issues with these disorders require a slightly different approach. Similarly, if you realize while reading through this book that your child's anxiety extends far beyond their sleep issues (e.g., being fearful in new and/or familiar situations or expressing significant worry throughout the day), then it is worth considering a visit with a psychologist. We typically consider *interference with daily functioning* to help determine whether the anxiety is developmentally appropriate or a passing phase. That is, consider whether your child's anxiety is preventing them from doing things they want to do (e.g., going on a playdate) or from doing things they need to do (e.g., attending school or doctor appointments).

We are often asked: "Which should be tackled first, sleep or anxiety?" Unfortunately, 10 different specialists will give you 10 different answers because there is no one-size-fits-all approach. There is research to support both that treating sleep alone can help improve anxiety (de Bruin et al., 2018) and that treating anxiety alone can help improve sleep (Clementi et al., 2016; for more on the relationship between sleep and mental health conditions, see Johnson et al., 2006). However, it can be helpful to think of your child's struggles as a hierarchy. Maybe you start with the item that is easiest to tackle (or the low hanging fruit), or maybe you start with the item that causes the most interference with family life (the fruit a little higher up the tree). Regardless, if your child seems to have symptoms of anxiety that extend past bedtime, it can't hurt to get a professional opinion on where to start.

A psychologist who specifically works with children can help parse out whether the symptoms are more general (e.g., generalized anxiety) or more specific (e.g., separation anxiety). Although both issues, and many other anxiety disorders, can impact bedtime, it can sometimes be helpful to equip your child, and yourself, with ways to respond to the anxiety during the daytime hours *before* working on how it impacts their sleep. Ideally, a provider who is also well versed in pediatric sleep can help you tackle the issues at hand. It can be a bit overwhelming to try to find the right provider for your child. We suggest starting with your child's pediatrician or school counselor, because they often have lists of therapists that they can personally recommend. Once you have connected with someone, it is important to ask about their treatment approach and their experience with treating sleep. Most therapists will do an initial intake appointment, sometimes prior to even meeting the child, and this can be a really good time to ask questions about what the treatment will look like. Also, it is important to remember that if you start working with someone and it does not feel like it is going in the direction you thought, you can and should discuss this with the therapist. They may be able to shift their approach or can connect you with someone else if not.

One other thing to consider is when to have your child be a more active participant in the therapeutic process. It can be beneficial for a child to meet with the therapist, in addition to their parent doing work on shifting their responses to behaviors, particularly if the child is struggling with emotional expression or does not appear to have adequate coping skills. Additionally, some children like to feel that they are part of the process and want to have a voice in the decisions that are being made. Including a child in this process can certainly increase buy-in. In addition, helping them to see that this is a team approach, and not just a mandate being placed on them, can decrease some children's anxiety around changes that may be coming. It can often be beneficial for the therapist to at least meet your child, and together you can determine what approach would be most beneficial.

CLOSING THOUGHTS

In closing, we want to give you some labeled praise! You have done a wonderful job and worked incredibly hard to get more sleep for your entire family. You have just given your child the gift of good sleep for years to come, in addition to physical health, mental health, and academic success. Okay, sufficient sleep might not guarantee perfection in all of these areas, but you have joined us in recognizing that sleep is an incredibly important piece of the puzzle. You did good work and now have a workbook full of tips, tricks, and your own plans and reflections should you ever need a refresher!

REFERENCES

Adolescent Sleep Working Group, Committee on Adolescence, & Council on School Health. (2014). School start times for adolescents. *Pediatrics*, *134*(3), 642–649. https://doi.org/10.1542/peds.2014-1697

Agency for Healthcare Research and Quality. (2022). Child and adolescent mental health. In *National Healthcare Quality and Disparities Report*. https://www.ncbi.nlm.nih.gov/books/NBK587174/

American Academy of Pediatrics. (2022, October 24). *American Academy of Pediatrics updates safe sleep recommendations: Back is best*. https://www.aap.org/en/news-room/news-releases/aap/2022/american-academy-of-pediatrics-updates-safe-sleep-recommendations-back-is-best/

American Academy of Sleep Medicine. (2016, June 13). *AAP endorses new recommendations on sleep times*. https://publications.aap.org/aapnews/news/6630/AAP-endorses-new-recommendations-on-sleep-times

American Medical Association. (2016, June 14). *AMA supports delayed school start times to improve adolescent wellness*. https://www.ama-assn.org/press-center/press-releases/ama-supports-delayed-school-start-times-improve-adolescent-wellness

Baattaiah, B. A., Alharbi, M. D., Babteen, N. M., Al-Maqbool, H. M., Babgi, F. A., & Albatati, A. A. (2023). The relationship between fatigue, sleep quality, resilience, and the risk of postpartum depression: An emphasis on maternal mental health. *BMC Psychology*, *11*(1), 10. https://doi.org/10.1186/s40359-023-01043-3

Bear, G. G., Slaughter, J. C., Mantz, L. S., & Farley-Ripple, E. (2017). Rewards, praise, and punitive consequences: Relations with intrinsic and extrinsic motivation. *Teaching and Teacher Education*, *65*, 10–20. https://doi.org/10.1016/j.tate.2017.03.001

Beebe, D. W., Rose, D., & Amin, R. (2010). Attention, learning, and arousal of experimentally sleep-restricted adolescents in a simulated classroom. *Journal of Adolescent Health*, *47*(5), 523–525. https://doi.org/10.1016/j.jadohealth.2010.03.005

Beebe, D. W., Simon, S., Summer, S., Hemmer, S., Strotman, D., & Dolan, L. M. (2013). Dietary intake following experimentally restricted sleep in adolescents. *Sleep*, *36*(6), 827–834. https://doi.org/10.5665/sleep.2704

Bin-Hasan, S., Kapur, K., Rakesh, K., & Owens, J. (2020). School start time change and motor vehicle crashes in adolescent drivers. *Journal of Clinical Sleep Medicine*, *16*(3), 371–376. https://doi.org/10.5664/jcsm.8208

Canapari, C. (2019). *It's never too late to sleep train: The low-stress way to high-quality sleep for babies, kids, and parents*. Rodale.

Clementi, M. A., Alfano, C. A., Holly, L. E., & Pina, A. A. (2016). Sleep-related outcomes following early intervention for childhood anxiety. *Journal of Child and Family Studies*, *25*(11), 3270–3277. https://doi.org/10.1007/s10826-016-0478-6

Cohen, P. A., Avula, B., Wang, Y. H., Katragunta, K., & Khan, I. (2023). Quantity of melatonin and CBD in melatonin gummies sold in the US. *JAMA*, *329*(16), 1401–1402. https://doi.org/10.1001/jama.2023.2296

de Bruin, E. J., Bögels, S. M., Oort, F. J., & Meijer, A. M. (2018). Improvements of adolescent psychopathology after insomnia treatment: Results from a randomized controlled trial over 1 year. *Journal of Child Psychology*, *59*(5), 509. https://doi.org/10.1111/jcpp.12834

Erland, L. A., & Saxena, P. K. (2017). Melatonin natural health products and supplements: Presence of serotonin and significant variability of melatonin content. *Journal of Clinical Sleep Medicine*, *13*(2), 275–281. https://doi.org/10.5664/jcsm.6462

Gruber, R., Cassoff, J., Frenette, S., Wiebe, S., & Carrier, J. (2012). Impact of sleep extension and restriction on children's emotional lability and impulsivity. *Pediatrics*, *130*(5), e1155–e1161. https://doi.org/10.1542/peds.2012-0564

Hagenauer, M. H., Perryman, J. I., Lee, T. M., & Carskadon, M. A. (2009). Adolescent changes in the homeostatic and circadian regulation of sleep. *Developmental Neuroscience*, *31*(4), 276–284. https://doi.org/10.1159/000216538

Hiscock, H., Bayer, J., Gold, L., Hampton, A., Ukoumunne, O. C., & Wake, M. (2007). Improving infant sleep and maternal mental health: A cluster randomised trial. *Archives of Disease in Childhood*, *92*(11), 952–958. https://doi.org/10.1136/adc.2006.099812

Honaker, S. M., Schwichtenberg, A. J., Kreps, T. A., & Mindell, J. A. (2018). Real-world implementation of infant behavioral sleep interventions: Results of a parental survey. *Journal of Pediatrics*, *199*, 106–111. https://doi.org/10.1016/j.jpeds.2018.04.009

Johnson, E. O., Roth, T., & Breslau, N. (2006). The association of insomnia with anxiety disorders and depression: Exploration of the direction of risk. *Journal of Psychiatric Research*, *40*(8), 700–708. https://doi.org/10.1016/j.jpsychires.2006.07.008

Migueis, D. P., Lopes, M. C., Casella, E., Soares, P. V., Soster, L., & Spruyt, K. (2023). Attention deficit hyperactivity disorder and restless leg syndrome across the lifespan: A systematic review and meta-analysis. *Sleep Medicine Reviews*, *69*, 101770. https://doi.org/10.1016/j.smrv.2023.101770

Mindell, J. A., & Barrett, K. M. (2002). Nightmares and anxiety in elementary-aged children: Is there a relationship? *Child: Care, Health and Development*, *28*(4), 317–322. https://doi.org/10.1046/j.1365-2214.2002.00274.x

Mindell, J. A., Li, A. M., Sadeh, A., Kwon, R., & Goh, D. Y. (2015). Bedtime routines for young children: A dose-dependent association with sleep outcomes. *Sleep*, *38*(5), 717–722. https://doi.org/10.5665/sleep.4662

Mindell, J. A., Meltzer, L. J., Carskadon, M. A., & Chervin, R. D. (2009). Developmental aspects of sleep hygiene: Findings from the 2004 National Sleep Foundation Sleep in America Poll. *Sleep Medicine*, *10*(7), 771–779. https://doi.org/10.1016/j.sleep.2008.07.016

Moon, R. Y. (2022, June 21). *New safe sleep recommendations can help pediatricians guide families*. AAP News. https://publications.aap.org/aapnews/news/20619/New-safe-sleep-recommendations-can-help

Moon, R. Y., Tanabe, K. O., Yang, D. C., Young, H. A., & Hauck, F. R. (2012). Pacifier use and SIDS: Evidence for a consistently reduced risk. *Maternal and Child Health Journal*, *16*(3), 609–614. https://doi.org/10.1007/s10995-011-0793-x

Moore, M., & Meltzer, L. J. (2008). The sleepy adolescent: Causes and consequences of sleepiness in teens. *Paediatric Respiratory Reviews*, 9(2), 114–120. https://doi.org/10.1016/j.prrv.2008.01.001

National Sleep Foundation. (2020, October 1). *How much sleep do you really need?* https://www.thensf.org/how-many-hours-of-sleep-do-you-really-need/

O'Brien, E. M., & Mindell, J. A. (2005). Sleep and risk-taking behavior in adolescents. *Behavioral Sleep Medicine*, 3(3), 113–133. https://doi.org/10.1207/s15402010bsm0303_1

Pennestri, M.-H., Burdayron, R., Kenny, S., Béliveau, M.-J., & Dubois-Comtois, K. (2020). Sleeping through the night or through the nights? *Sleep Medicine*, 76, 98–103. https://doi.org/10.1016/j.sleep.2020.10.005

Pennestri, M.-H., Laganière, C., Bouvette-Turcot, A.-A., Pokhvisneva, I., Steiner, M., Meaney, M. J., & Gaudreau, H. (2018). Uninterrupted infant sleep, development, and maternal mood. *Pediatrics*, 142(6), e20174330. https://doi.org/10.1542/peds.2017-4330

Rzepka-Migut, B., & Paprocka, J. (2020). Efficacy and safety of melatonin treatment in children with autism spectrum disorder and attention-deficit/hyperactivity disorder—A review of the literature. *Brain Sciences*, 10(4), 219. https://doi.org/10.3390/brainsci10040219

Sawyer, H., & Taie, S. (2020). *Start time for U.S. public high schools* [Data point]. NCES 2020-006. National Center for Education Statistics.

Sprajcer, M., Dawson, D., Kosmadopoulos, A., Sach, E. J., Crowther, M. E., Sargent, C., & Roach, G. D. (2023). How tired is too tired to drive? A systematic review assessing the use of prior sleep duration to detect driving impairment. *Nature and Science of Sleep*, 15, 175–206. https://doi.org/10.2147/NSS.S392441

St-Onge, M., Mercier, P., & De Koninck, J. (2009). Imagery rehearsal therapy for frequent nightmares in children. *Behavioral Sleep Medicine*, 7(2), 81–98. https://doi.org/10.1080/15402000902762360

Tham, E. K., Schneider, N., & Broekman, B. F. (2017). Infant sleep and its relation with cognition and growth: A narrative review. *Nature and Science of Sleep*, 9, 135–149. https://doi.org/10.2147/NSS.S125992

U.S. Centers for Disease Control and Prevention. (2020, September 10). *Sleep in middle and high school students.* https://www.cdc.gov/healthyschools/features/students-sleep.htm

Watson, N. F., Martin, J. L., Wise, M. S., Carden, K. A., Kirsch, D. B., Kristo, D. A., Malhotra, R. K., Olson, E. J., Ramar, K., Rosen, I. M., Rowley, J. A., Weaver, T. E., & Chervin, R. D. (2017). Delaying middle school and high school start times promotes student health and performance: An American Academy of Sleep Medicine position statement. *Journal of Clinical Sleep Medicine, 13*(4), 623–625. https://doi.org/10.5664/jcsm.6558

Williamson, A. A., Leichman, E. S., Walters, R. M., & Mindell, J. A. (2019). Caregiver-perceived sleep outcomes in toddlers sleeping in cribs versus beds. *Sleep Medicine, 54,* 16–21. https://doi.org/10.1016/j.sleep.2018.10.012

INDEX

ABOUT THE AUTHORS

Andrea C. Roth, PsyD, is a licensed clinical psychologist and the clinical director of Thriving Minds Behavioral Health in Livonia, Michigan, a pediatric group practice that specializes in the treatment of children with a variety of mental health diagnoses. Dr. Roth is a trained cognitive–behavioral therapist and specializes in the treatment of anxiety-based disorders, including generalized anxiety disorder, obsessive–compulsive disorder and selective mutism. She also runs the student training program for behavioral sleep treatment at Thriving Minds. Prior to her clinical career, Dr. Roth worked in sleep research at the University of Wisconsin and Henry Ford Hospital in Detroit. Dr. Roth has served as a research consultant at Henry Ford Hospital and has many published articles within the sleep field.

Allison Shale, PsyD, is the owner and director of Shale Psychology, LLC, an outpatient mental health practice in northern New Jersey, focused on treating children and adolescents with a range of emotional and behavioral difficulties. Dr. Shale is trained as a cognitive–behavioral therapist (CBT) and specializes in working with children with ADHD and mood disorders such as anxiety and depression. Additionally, she is certified in parent–child interaction therapy (PCIT) and does a tremendous amount of parent training and behavior management work. Dr. Shale is active within her community, providing talks and workshops at local schools, libraries, and nearby treatment facilities. Outside of her clinical work, she supervises advanced graduate students who are in the process of earning their PCIT certification.

Shelby F. Harris, Psyd, DBSM, is a clinical psychologist and sleep specialist in private practice in New York. She is board certified in behavioral sleep medicine and treats a wide variety of sleep, anxiety, and depression issues using evidence-based, nonmedication treatments. Her self-help book *The Women's Guide to Overcoming Insomnia* was published in 2019 by W. W. Norton Books. Dr. Harris holds an academic appointment as a clinical associate professor at the Albert Einstein College of Medicine in Neurology and Psychiatry. Before going into private practice, she was the longstanding director of the Behavioral Sleep Medicine Program at the Sleep–Wake Disorders Center at Montefiore Medical Center in New York City. Dr. Harris has been an invited columnist for *The New York Times,* and is frequently in the media including *The New Yorker, The Washington Post,* CBS Mornings, the Today Show, and The Drew Barrymore Show.